Developing Trust & Collaboration between Law Enforcement and the Black Community:

A Post Trayvon Martin Program Evaluation

BY

Dr. Benjamin Roberts, LMFT

Bachelor of Arts, Lipscomb University, 1982

Master of Arts, Harding School of Theology, 2004

Master of Arts, Liberty University, 2015

Doctor of Ministry in Family Therapy, Amridge University

Developing Trust & Collaboration between Law Enforcement and the Black Community:
A Post Trayvon Martin Program Evaluation

Dr. Benjamin Roberts, Jr.

© 2021

Published by BRJ Publishers
Layout by www.diverseskillscenter.com

Printed in the United States of America
U.S. Copyright No. 1-9674580434
ISBN: 978-0-578-79745-8

Abstract

The objective of this work was to evaluate a three-year-old outreach program developed by an African American church to enhance trust with the local police. This evaluation answers basic questions about the program's usefulness. Assessment of gathered information will be used to improve program goals. This evaluation will find out "what is working" that will enhance trust from police and church members perspectives. Qualitative research by means of two focus groups is used to determine strengths, weaknesses, and possibilities for the program and collect meaningful answers from the questions of: Has the outreach program of this church helped develop trust with the police department? What is the role of the police department in helping the outreach program build trust? How does the ecological systems theory (collaboration) assist in helping the outreach program build trust?

Dedicated to:

My wife and best friend, Leota Roberts, who has been by my side over the years.

with love, patience, and understanding.

This book would not have been completed without you.

Acknowledgements:

Paige Brown, Mayor of Gallatin, Tennessee for her ongoing support of the Church. Ms. Brown has been to many of our activities and has been guest speaker for our yearly events. Our City has improved under her leadership.

Chief Don Bandy and the entire Police Department in Gallatin, Tennessee for their continuous support in the community. They have assisted the Church in many activities and ensured protection and safety over the years.

The Elders from the West Eastland Church and Christ and the entire church for their encouragement and support during this study. The church has continuously participated in the many church activities that has opened the communication between the community and Law Enforcement.

A Special thanks to each of the participants who gave their time and opinions to help open up the communication between Law Enforcement and the Black community.

Table of Contents

Chapter 2:

WHAT THE LITERATURE IS SAYING 40

Chapter 3:

RESEARCH METHODOLOGY 90

LIST OF TABLES FIGURES

LIST OF TABLES

INTRODUCTION

Drinking my morning coffee while browsing the morning news on television, I see yet another protest located, this time in Charlotte, North Carolina. A police officer has once again shot and killed an African American man. These unfavorable encounters are becoming all too common in the streets of our country. Besides the protesting and the violence, Charlotte Police Chief Kerr Putney, an African American, appears to struggle with words as he reaches for that part of him that has to be politically correct and represent all of his officers on one hand, and on the other hand dismiss his awareness that the police have killed another man of his race. The challenges that exist between the police and the African American community will continue to get worse, and there will be no changes in their attitudes unless the two groups can appreciate each other.

As a practicing marriage and family therapist, I believe that the whole is greater than the sum of its parts. I want to introduce this book by looking at the African American community from a system's perspective. My theory, not yet empirical data, is that the abusive process of dehumanization of African Americans from the time of slavery until the present has created a desecrated system that consists of at least five parts. Each part depends on the other to cope and survive in an inauspicious perceived environment. Furthermore, the role of these parts is more significant than individuals who may be detected being in more than one role of involvement.

The first is the dominant part—what I call the "citizen." The citizen comes from all socioeconomic clusters within the African American system. The citizen's function is to demonstrate that African Americans are no different from any other group in this diverse country. The citizen goes to work daily, takes pride in the culture, loves family, loves the country, and looks well adjusted. The citizen consists of different family structures. This group slashes down stereotypes that are often cited by the dominant race.

Second, the "traitor" part of the system functions as a testing ground to see how well the dominant race is accepting the African American system. This group will be observed by repeating phrases from the dominant race about the African American system. Republican presidential candidate Ben Carson and

Milwaukee County, Wisconsin, Sheriff David Clarke are examples of traitors. Furthermore, most African Americans in the Republican party would be considered traitors. The other parts of the system often observe the traitor part intensively to determine how safe it is to trust the dominant race.

The dominant race appears to be less intimidated by this group and more receptive. This may be true because the dominant race does not see the role of the traitor. The traitor's role is to manipulate and take advantage of the dominant race. The traitor may be the most narcissistic part of the African American system.

Third, the "protestor" part of the African American system functions to bring attention to any wrong that has come upon the system. Due to the police cruelty toward African American males, the protestors have come out by the hundreds to protest police departments in several major cities in the country. There may be some citizens in this group, but it appears to be made up of many college students, sympathizers of different ethnic and racial groups, and young professional African Americans. The dehumanized system depends on the protestor to make a robust proclamation about any injustice or threat that African Americans may be experiencing.

Fourth, the "calvary" part of the African American system functions to bring violence when the system feels that the protestors are not being heard or taken seriously. From my observation, it appears that members of this group are willing to sacrifice their future, or maybe their lives, to bring immediate attention to the threat that is being experienced by the system. Perhaps members of this group have the least to lose, with a history of recorded criminal behavior. The calvary is an incredibly important part of the system's survival during times of injustice because members of the calvary may pay the ultimate price of death for the dehumanized system. The calvary also exists to shine a light on the consequences of what has happened socially, politically, and economically to African Americans in this country.

Finally, the "leader" part of the African American system functions to navigate and explain why the different parts of the system are responding a certain way under certain circumstances. Members of this group will be observed commenting on television and on social media. These may be politicians, ministers, athletes, celebrities, and other key figures in the community. It is important to remember that each of these personalities is important for the African American system to cope due to many years of abusive dehumanization.

There are many similarities between what victims of abuse have experienced and that of the African American system. Furthermore, there is documentation that shows how individuals who have experienced extreme abuse have several personalities for survival. For example, the dissociative identity disorder is believed to be a complex psychological condition that is likely activated by numerous influences, including trauma throughout primary childhood, or constant physical, sexual, or emotional abuse. This condition is similar to what the African American system has experienced from the abusive process of dehumanization.

The purpose of this book is to share a three year research of developing trust between police and the African American community, and to initiate the process of changing the distrusting attitudes that exist between the police and the African American system. I discuss the history of the police and the African American system in this country. Most of the book consist of the research conducted, results discovered, and possible solutions to the problem. The first section of this book will be concerned with the history of the police and the African American system.

History of Police and African Americans

Slave Patrol Era

Slave patrols started in South Carolina during the early 1700s and dispensed through the entire thirteen colonies, continuing past the American Revolution. Because the populace of slaves boomed, with the creation of the cotton gin especially, so did worries of slave uprisings and resistance. The advancement of slave patrols began when another method of slave control did not implant slave obedience and monitoring. Their biggest concern had been slaves on the plantations since that is where slave populations had been highest. Initially, incentives such as tobacco and cash were given as rewards for whites to become more vigilant in the capture of runaway slaves. When this process proved not to be effective, slave patrols were established to control slave behavior (Hadden, 2003).

According to McNair (2009), exclusive in the Georgia slave code of 1750, parallel to those of other colonies, was its unease with the misconduct of whites, and not that of Black bondsmen. The only such provision that applied to Blacks' behavior—and it applied to whites as well—outlawed interracial sex and marriage. There were no embargoes against slave criminality of any kind.

Furthermore, rules were employed to regulate the actions of both whites and Blacks. Slaves who were stumbling about without authorization had to return to their owners, as declared in the slave code of laws. Retribution for runaway slaves could be expected, if not demanded, by statute. Sometimes there were penalties placed on slave owners if harsh punishment was not executed. Slaves were put through interrogation, examinations, along with other types of provocation. Also, it was not uncommon for beatings and whippings for both noncompliant and obedient slaves could be expected, and often a lot more than beatings and floggings; nevertheless, slaves feared the risk of being positioned on the auction away from family and friends (Hadden, 2003).

This meant becoming divided from their families, who had been the most extensive support in dealing with their scenario. If captured by patrols and returned to their masters, becoming situated on the auction block was an option for slave owners who did not want to manage their noncompliant slaves. During these times, slaves were frequently neglected and mistreated despite having the authorization to travel.

Jim Crow Era

Following the American Civil War, most Southern states passed laws that discriminated against African Americans. These laws and regulations became known as Jim Crow laws. In the United States during this period, social and racial mobility was a revolving door that maintained a relatively small number of more privileged positions that could be gained, as well as lost, over the course of one's life. These findings call into question much of the received wisdom regarding the rigidness of racial distinctions in the United States and further complicate comparisons of the moving targets that are race relations in the United States (Saperstein & Gullickson, 2013).

Lynching was commonly used as an extralegal method of the reprimand of African Americans during the Jim Crow era. It was fated by African American leaders such as W. E. B. Du Bois and

Ida B. Wells in newspaper articles such as "Thirty Years of Lynching in the United States: 1889–1918," published by the NAACP in 1919. Lynching was not restricted to the South, nor were African Americans the only victims, evidenced by the lynching of Leo Frank, a Jewish pencil factory manager in Marietta, Georgia, in 1915 (Lewis & Lewis, 2009. p. 122). Unfortunately, many times police officers were a part of the lynch mobs that would subdue and lynch African Americans.

Jim Crow laws incorporated laws and regulations that discriminated against Black people in this country. Many of these statutes were centered around "colored" people in regard to the issue of attendance in public areas schools and the usage of services such as restaurants, theaters, resorts, cinemas, and general public baths. Buses and trains were also segregated, and, in lots of states, the relationships between whites and African American individuals were restricted. The laws were to be enforced by the police. The police had taken an oath to uphold laws that were discriminatory to Black people. African American people who violated a state's transportation segregation policies were arrested and fined. In 1956, African Americans, directed by Dr. Martin Luther King Jr. and Rosa Parks, structured the successful Montgomery bus boycott.

CHAPTER 1

RESEARCH FOCUS

The Research was focused on an in-depth study of a collaboration between the Boston police and a group of pastors who reported an increase in the injustice of police toward African Americans (Brunson et al., 2015). An increasing number of cases has been filed, wherein police officers shoot unarmed African American males in the United States (Brunson et al., 2015). There is a need for the church to do more in developing trust between police and the African American community. This research examined the effectiveness of an African American church outreach program created to develop trust with the local police.

"Post Trayvon Martin" refers to the period after the death of Trayvon Martin. On 26 February 2012, Martin, an African American teenager, was shot and killed by a Hispanic man named George Zimmerman. After a sixteen-and-a-half-hour deliberation, a jury of Zimmerman's peers found him not guilty of Martin's death (Yancy & Jones, 2013). After Martin's death, the news media highlighted several shootings and killings of African American men by police. This research takes place during a heightened awareness of trust issues between the African American community and police.

Personal Background Story

I am an African American minister who has preached in the Church of Christ for forty years. Additionally, I am a licensed marital and family therapist. I have served as the minister for the West Eastland Church of Christ in Gallatin, Tennessee, for twenty-five years. There was an incident in Gallatin of a police officer shooting and killing an African American woman on April 7, 2016. According to Karakurt and Silver (2014), one of the preeminent approaches to address concerns is to use the Family Systems Therapy orientation. My being an African American minister and a family therapist qualifies me to address this research from two perspectives. System theory suggests that when seeking counseling for an event, clients are unable to be understood or assisted when broken off independently, but rather should be kept as a part of the family unit. By doing so, the client has a better chance of seeking and getting what they need to improve their condition. Since the church is the center of the African American community and is regarded as a large extended family, it would be logical to apply this setting and structure of helping to rebuild the relationship of trust and mutual respect between the community and the police (Combrinck-Graham, 2014).

Focus of the Proposed Study

The focus of this study was to evaluate a three-year-old church outreach program designed to develop trust between police and an African American church. The emphasis of the proposed analysis was to unearth experiences through the outreach program that have taken place between police and the church, then assess results. The proposed study evaluated the West Eastland Church of Christ outreach program, with the aim of discovering better ways the two parties can communicate so that both sides can maintain a relationship that incorporates trust and mutual respect.

Congregational Setting and Structure

The African American church and police for this research are located in a city with the population of about 45,000 located approximately thirty miles from a metropolitan town. The church outreach program was evaluated for its effectiveness. The church focus group consisted of African Americans from different generations, and educational and socioeconomic groups. The police focus group consisted of white males, different ages, various years on the force, and diverse educational achievements.

Key Concepts

The study employs several key concepts in relation to trust issues between police and the African American church, which represents its community. Many of these concepts are related to one another in some fashion, yet they are distinct enough to contribute toward the study in unique ways. According to Boyd Franklin (2013), the church plays a crucial role in healing the issues between the community and police. The following section of the study presents the researcher's statement of the problem.

Statement of the Problem

I am the initiator of the West Eastland Church of Christ outreach program. All goals, expectations, and vision for the program are mine. This is a top-down organizational structure that has given no voice to police and church members. For the program to reach possibilities, it had to implement what police and church members believed they needed to build trust.

Business management understands the value of including employees in decision-making. The bottom-up management style helps the company grow. Crosby (1986) states the purpose of employee involvement is not to create a more friendly work environment, although that is a desirable by-product; its primary purpose is to improve productivity. The research allowed police and church members to give insight on the effectiveness of the program and ways it can be enhanced.

Need for the Study

The need for the study was to determine the effectiveness of the program and to determine if desired outcomes were met. The program has goals of building trust, strengthening communication, and increasing respect between police and the African American church. Without the study, there was no way to determine if these goals were being met. Also, funding institutions assess accountability through program effectiveness (Hernandez, 2000).

This study was to bring credibility to the program. An effective program of this sort could go a long way in helping build the relationship between police and the African American community.

Purpose of the Study

The purpose of this study was to evaluate an outreach program developed by an African American church to develop trust with the local police. The church's outreach program lasted for three years. The program was initiated when the church reached out to its local police to develop trust by providing a yearly appreciation lunch and collaborating in numerous community services. This study was to discover if the program is doing what it is designed to do. What are the possibilities for the program? How can the program be improved? What are the key factors in developing a better police-community alliance?

Significance of the Study

This program evaluation was to help determine if any significant changes have taken place between the two groups.

Formative evaluation was needed here to determine the practical role for this program (Scriven, 1996). What are the changes that have occurred? What are the impacts of these changes? What can the church do differently? What can the police do differently? Further, these outcomes are essential in developing short-term and long-term goals. Strategic goal setting and planning are the foundations for the success of any program (Hartwig, 2000). The information gathered from this project will be used to enhance its strengths, correct its weaknesses, and build upon its next opportunities. Furthermore, the extended goal is to develop a curriculum that can be used by police and churches to enhance collaborative efforts in developing trust between police and the African American community.

How the Goal Will Be Achieved

Two focus groups were used to solicit information from participants. One group was officers from the police, and one group was members of the church. Ultimately, the church was the prime tool in helping bridge the gap between the African American community and the police, but with lots of information from the police and the church (Moore & Neiderhiser, 2014). The purpose of the study is relevant as ever, with the current condition of the relationship between the groups. The study was an honest attempt to evaluate and develop a program to build trust and to establish a positive working relationship between both groups.

Research Questions

To effectively evaluate this outreach program, research questions were used as tools to conduct the research. The questions were used to determine the effectiveness of the outreach program and evaluate ways of making the program more efficient.

1. How has the outreach program of this church help built?
2. What was the role of this church in helping the outreach program build trust?
3. What was the role of the police department in helping the outreach program build trust?
4. does the ecological systems theory (collaboration) assist in helping the outreach program build trust?

Delimitations of the Study

The research did not examine if trust issues are worse since an African American teenager, Trayvon Martin, was shot and killed by a Hispanic man named George Zimmerman. Also, did not focus on slavery or what white people and African Americans think of each other. This was a program evaluation. There are specific boundaries that defined the scope and purpose of the study. For example, the geographically defined area where the proposed study occurred is a good choice because typically the news media and other sources tend to associate the trust issues between the police and the African American church community with the large and urban areas (Brunson & Weitzer, 2011). The study focuses on a specific small town in Tennessee that the researcher is familiar with, therefore demonstrating that the problems are not limited to the cities in the United States.

Additionally, the chosen scope of this study not only utilizes the ministry and counseling theories, but there is also a historical lens applied. The historical lens is applied to gain a clearer understanding of the background of the problem. Without the addition of the historical lens, the study loses its merits on focus, as there has to be a clear understanding of the history of mistrust between the white police officers and the African American church (Brunson & Weitzer, 2011).

Definition of Key Terms

Before proceeding with other aspects of the study, it is significant to give working definitions of key terms and phrases that will be used regularly. This prevents the information from being improperly interpreted and communicated. Following is a brief list of the key terms and phrases involved in the study and their accepted working definitions:

- *Trust* is fundamentally an attitude based on beliefs, feelings, and implying expectations and dispositions. It also implies a sense of the other's competence (Govier, 1997). The definition of trust in this research project is in essence an attitude of positive expectation between police and the church, a sense that actions are basically well intentioned and unlikely to do harm. To trust someone is to expect that he/she will act well, that he/she will take one's interests into account and do no harm (Govier, 1998).

- *Church/Church of Christ* used in this research refers to the Church of Christ (A Capella) that was normally viewed as the conservative part of the North American Stone-Campbell Movement formally recognized in 1906 (Williams, 2012).

- *The ecological systems theory* was developed by Urie Bronfenbrenner. He identified five environmental systems with which an individual interacts. The collaboration of these systems influences developmental growth of individuals (Rosa & Tudge, 2013).

- The *Family Systems Model,* according to Karakurt and Silver (2014), states that a client is apt to achieve better results seeking therapy in a family setting than individually, specifically when the issue is centered on the family or the group with which the patient identifies.

- *Community policing* is a unique style of policing that involves the community and presents the officers as partners in safety, rather than typical aggressive authority figures that community members fear (Bain, Robinson, & Conser, 2014, August 12).

- *Black Defiance Theology* is a style of ministering to the African American church that dates back to the period of slavery, when there was defiance against the "white culture" (Clardy, 2011). Black pastors are considered celebrities, and these communities are looked upon them for leadership in matters of politics and social justice, stating that their behavior greatly influences the rest of the church family.

- The *African American church*, according to Nelson and Nelson (1975), is the focal point of Black communities in America. These churches and their leadership should be more involved in changing the mindset of the members of the church community where the mistrust of the police is concerned.

Pastoral counseling/Christian counseling for the current study is defined as the process by which the pastors and ministers give counsel to church members to help resolve issues, including the mistrust of the police (Karakurt & Silver, 2014).

- *Social media reporting*, according to Dowler (2003), involves online, print, and televised media sources that report the news items about crimes and other social issues, which for the current study is the broken relationship between the police and the African American community.

Research Methodology

The study was an evaluation of an African American church's outreach program to build trust with the local police. There are three options when choosing a research methodology: quantitative, qualitative, and mixed methods. Quantitative methodology is appropriate for studies that involve the identification of possible significant relationships between two or more variables, which can be independent, dependent, or controlled (Mertens, 2014).

Qualitative methodology is used when the purpose of the research is to explore, investigate, explain, or describe a phenomenon within an uncontrolled environment, using data about perceptions, experiences, and behaviors of individuals (Major & Savin-Baden, 2010). Mixed method is used when the research question has both a qualitative and quantitative component to address the problem.

Rationale for Research Method

As stated above, the qualitative methodology is used when the purpose of the research is to explore, investigate, explain, or describe a phenomenon within an uncontrolled environment, using data about perceptions, experiences, and behaviors of individuals (Major & Savin-Baden, 2010). A qualitative research method utilizing a focus group will be used to evaluate this program.

Focus groups provide insights into how people think and provide a deeper understanding of the trust issues between the two groups.

The group is focused on the sense that it involves some collective action and is dissimilar from the larger category of group interview by the explicit use of the group interaction as research data (Kitzinger, 1994). Good interviewing skills are needed to conduct a focus group. Focus groups provide an opportunity to hear participants and observe body language. The researcher observes how the participants interact and react to one another. It is also less time-consuming and less expensive than other methods. However, some drawbacks to focus groups are their deficiency of anonymity and lack of participation by some. The interviewer may misinterpret nonverbals of participants, and inadvertently influence collected data (Kuhn, 2000), and interviewer biases can influence the outcome of the study if left unaddressed (Sorsa, Kiikkala, stedt-Kurki, 2015).

Sample Size/Research Process

Two groups were solicited for participation. One group was officers from the police, and one group was members of the church. Each group consisted of eight to ten members and each session lasted for approximately ninety minutes. The interviews took place at the police department and church classroom. Two or more groups are recommended with focus groups, and small sample sizes are legitimate in qualitative research (Carlsen & Glenton, 2011). Individuals who can provide the best information were asked to participate. Due to Gallatin having a small police department, the goal was to have any officer participate who is not in a supervisory position. It is worth noting that some of the officers had not spent the same amount time involved in the outreach program, and some not at all. However, information still could be gained on how to improve the program. I was aware that this was a convenience sampling. According to Emerson (2015), convenience sampling helps researchers obtain the number of participants they desire, but the way the participants are gathered can easily influence the results by introducing unexpected or uncontrolled factors. Any of these factors might have an impact on what the study is investigating.

The goal was to see what was working or not working in the outreach programs and identify areas of improvement from the eyes of the local police and church members. The chief of police granted permission for recruitment and data collection of officers. Criteria used for church member participation was ages twenty to seventy-five. The goal was to have three generations of interaction. Church members had to be able to read and drive. Driving is important because this is where a lot unfavorable interacting begins or has happened between the two groups. For the church, the shepherds granted permission for recruitment and data collection of church members.

The questions for the focus groups were semi-structured open-ended. Therefore, the main instrument used was an interview guide. Interview questions were developed based on existing literature and in alignment with the research questions. Each research question had at least three corresponding items in the interview guide. A digital recorder was used to collect conversation in the focus group, along with my own notes that captured nonverbal expression of group members. The audio recording was transcribed into Microsoft Word (or Microsoft Excel), as that is what is required for conducting the analyses via software (typically NVivo or MAXQDA). My notes, along with the software, were used to convert data into information and knowledge.

Review of Literature

Currently, there is a significant amount of literature available supporting trust issues that exist between police and the African American community. However, there is not much information written by the Church of Christ on this subject. Later, I discuss what the literature states about the history of trust issues between police and the African American community. Also, I compare and contrast with my research what the literature articulates about trust in general and the challenge of differentiating between trust and trust worthiness.

Other reviewed literature was concerned with what has been written in regard to the role of the police and the church collaborating to serve the community better. I discuss what the literature says and how these findings compare and contrast to my research. Finally, I observe the police and the African American community as two interacting systems and discuss how the literature says the family systems theory can be applied.

Sennett (2012) suggests that the spirit of cooperation has to be present to initiate successful changes to repair the current trust issues between the two parties. This program evaluation gave insight into how to fix this broken relationship. The first move could be taken from either of the groups. An African American church has reached across and extended a hand of fellowship. The church's outreach program has the potential the benefit both police and community.

Through the outreach program, the study unearthed experiences that were taking place between police and the church, then assessed the results. The study evaluated the outreach program, with the aim of discovering better ways the two parties could communicate so that both sides could maintain a relationship that incorporates trust and mutual respect. The next chapter discuss in detailed literature review associated with this project.

CHAPTER 2

WHAT THE LITERATURE IS SAYING

The objective of this literature review is to discuss and define different types of trust and investigate trust issues between African Americans and police. This chapter will examine the literature on collaboration between communities and police and explore what the literature says about the police's ability to do their job and African Americans being able to trust that police have their best interest in mind. The literature discuss how trust relates to issues between police and the Black community. In addition, this chapter demonstrates, through a review of literature, that police may not be unfair toward African Americans in general, but that this is relative to the high-crime areas in which many African Americans reside.

History of the Problem

Since Reconstruction, there has been evident mistrust between police and the African American community. With the church being the cultural center of the African American community, many believe that involvement of the church and its officials are the ultimate solution to repairing the damaged relationship between these two groups (MacDonald & Stokes, 2006). African American history has established the church's role in the community. The church is not only the center of cultural and spiritual life in the community but also a pseudo parent for the members of the extended family in this defined community (Clardy, 2011).

The role of the church identified in the African American society reflects upon the impact the church has had in resolving or further perpetuating the prevailing problem. Nelsen and Nelsen (1975) demonstrate in their book that the role of the church in the 1960s was to support its members and allow the members to congregate so they could contest the police as well as other authority figures that were determined to restrict the rights of African Americans. Churches in the African American communities became targets for white supremacy groups, and many were damaged or destroyed during the attacks in the Civil Rights Era (Nelsen & Nelsen, 1975). These churches, though damaged physically, became spiritual reminders to their members that if they stood together, they could unite against opposing forces, such as white police. It is an attitude that has been in place in the African American church for years.

What Is Trust?

Simpson (2012) states that trust is hard to define. However, he conveys that this does not mean that there is no philosophical understanding of the concept to be had, but the answer he recommends is that in existing communally, individuals must trust others to act supportively. "Thus 'trust' is an umbrella term under which plural notions cluster" (p. 551). Some actions point toward defining trust. The African American community and police need the support of each other to maintain law in the community.

This literature focuses on four major ways of conceptualizing trust. The purpose here is not to debate the pros and cons of each of these explanations, but to demonstrate their relevance to how trust can be defined to help evaluate and improve the West Eastland Church of Christ's outreach program. First, Annette Baier (1994) claims that "When I trust another, I depend on her goodwill toward me" (p. 99). Goodwill for this outreach program is best understood as *do not harm*. Media has exposed a painful history between the African American community and police. *Do not harm* as a goal can allow safer encounters between the two groups.

Second, Karen Jones (1996) expresses that the thought certainly inspires the trustee that the trusting individual is depending upon him or her. In the case of a traffic stop, the police officer is inspired that the African American driver depends upon him/her not to abuse authority and discretionary powers. Trust "is an attitude of optimism that the goodwill and competence of another will extend to cover the domain of our interaction with her, together with the expectation that the one trusted will be directly and favorably moved by the thought that we are counting on her" (Jones, 1996, p. 4).

Third, Richard Holton (1994) believes that one decides to trust. He is not convinced that belief is necessary to trust. He says certainly trust involves a certain state of mind, but it does not seem that it always involves a belief. "When you trust someone to do something, you rely on them to do it, and you regard that reliance in a certain way: you have a readiness to feel betrayal should it be disappointed, and gratitude should it be upheld" (p. 67). Holton is a beginning point to developing trust in the outreach program. Both groups can develop a state of mind to expect the other to do what is in the best interest of all involved.

Fourth, Russell Hardin (2002) believes that the trustee takes the trusting individual's interests into account. This aspect of trust is necessary to enhance the relationship between the African American community and police. As Johnson (2004) explains, "Many white law enforcement officials viewed the social movement of African Americans as a threat and treated it as a criminal act. Their beliefs mirrored those of whites (the author is speaking of Caucasian people) in the larger society who often viewed African Americans as social outcasts and criminals" (p. 119). African Americans must trust that their encounters with police are not about keeping them from progressing and having a part of the American dream.

The four major ways of conceptualizing trust involve individuals being accountable, reliable, and respectful toward one another. Reliability and respect between police and the church stand as the foundation of what the West Eastland Church of Christ sets as a goal for its outreach program.

Public Trust and Police

This research examines trust issues between police and an African American church. However, Tyler, Goff, and MacCoun (2015) report that public confidence and trust in the police have been deficient and that this problem has been intensified due to recent police shootings of unarmed Black men. According to this report, the trust of police is a concern for more people than African Americans, and that police validity is molded by the perception that police treat people with respect and fairness. The argument stated is that practices police use widely are many times viewed as being unfair and as such have resulted in a compromise of the population opinion of police as being a legal authority (Tyler et al., 2015).

When individuals perceive police as legitimate and appropriate legal authority, they are more likely to submit to the police in personal encounters and cooperate when given a directive by police (Tyler et al., 2015). Further, the view of the police being a legitimate authority is correlated according to the law in the lives of people as well as more community cooperating, crime reporting, identification of criminals, and willingness to serve in the capacity of witnesses and jurors (Tyler et al., 2015). However, Tyler (2016) importantly notes that community trust of police involves more than decreased crime and great service, but the experience of the interaction as well (p. 1). The procedural justice of the actions of police does matter to the public (Tyler, 2016).

For the police to influence the positive perception of the public there are critical elements that should be at focus including: (1) the participation of the public; (2) neutrality; (3) respect; and (4) trustworthiness. This means the involvement of the larger community in developing specific strategies in the management of social order and encouraging the acceptance of the public as well as their buy-in (Tyler et al., 2015).

Tyler, Goff, and MacCoun (2015) state that neutrality speaks of the engagement in decision-making that is transparent as well as being rule-based and thereby providing a demonstration that the policy of policing and the practices of policing are unbiased as well as fair. Respect means that citizens are treated with high levels of dignity and thereby communicating to the public that their rights are being respected. Finally, Tyler, Goff, and MacCoun (2015) cite trustworthiness as being understanding to individual needs and distresses and thereby indicating that police are sincere in their attempt to serve in the best interest for the individuals involved.

Cao, Lai, and Zhao (2012) state that trust in police "is related to one's position in the social stratification with the elite having higher confidence in the police and the poor having lower confidence" (p. 42). It is additionally reported by Cao, Lai, and Zhao (2012) that trust "in the police is part of a broader attitudinal complex or larger legal and political system" (p. 42). In other words, if the legal system is characterized by justice, then the population is more trusting of the police who patrol their community and neighborhoods.

Likewise, it is reported by the National Institute of Justice (2016) that research has demonstrated that people of minority races "are more likely than whites to view law enforcement with suspicion and distrust," with people of minority races reporting on a regular basis that they have been singled out disproportionately due to their ethnicity or race. It is reported that race impacts the level of satisfaction felt with police in an indirect manner and relation to "other factors, including the level of crime within one's neighborhood."

Criminal Justice and Trust

Gross, Possley, and Stephens (2017) reports that African Americans represent a mere 13 percent of the population of the United States, however, "a majority of innocent defendants wrongfully convicted of crimes and later exonerated" are represented by African American individuals (p. 2). It is additionally reported that for African Americans who are in prison for the crime of sexual assault that they are "three-and-a-half times more likely to be innocent than a white sexual assault convict"
(Gross, Possley & Stephens, 2017, p. 3).

The Associated Press – NORC Center for Public Affairs Research Brief (2015) reported that the relationship difficulties between African Americans and police officers in the United States are results of ongoing racial disunions in society's view of law enforcement and the criminal justice system. However, the brief (2015) states that policy, along with procedural changes, would be effective in bringing about a reduction in the tensions that exist between police and minority races, as well as successfully bringing about limitations in violent acts committed against civilians.

Findings reported from the study conducted by *The Associated Press – NORC Center for Public Affairs Research Brief* (2015) include that African Americans were found to be four times as likely to designate violence against citizens by police officers as a profoundly serious problem. Additionally, stated from the research findings is that more than 80 percent of African Americans report that police officers are far too quick to make use of force that is deadly and that this is even truer in regard to African Americans. (The Associated Press – NORC Center for Public Affairs Research, 2015). Of those participating in the study, 71 percent report that the use of body cameras by police would effectively deter violence being committed against civilians (The Associated Press – NORC Center for Public Affairs Research, 2015). The following chart shows the results of the study concerning the variations in the views of African Americans, whites, and Hispanics about the police

violence used against civilians.

Figure1

Differences in views of severity of police violence against the public

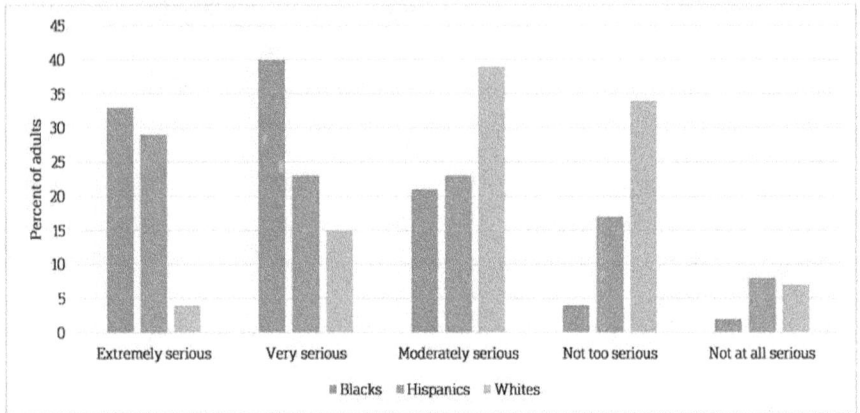

Question: How serious a problem do you think police violence against the PUBLIC is in the United States?

Source: The Associated Press – NORC Center for Public Affairs
Research (2015)

A total of 45 percent of Americans stated a belief that police use

force too quickly (The Associated Press – NORC Center for Public

Affairs Research, 2015). Additionally, reported is that 49 percent of

respondents stated a belief that an African American is more likely

to be on the receiving end of deadly force on the part of a police

officer (The Associated Press – NORC Center for Public Affairs

Research, 2015). The following chart shows the responses of

African Americans, whites, and Hispanics about their belief about whether deadly force is more likely to be used against an African

American both in general and in their communities.

Figure 2

Most blacks say police are more likely to use force against a black person

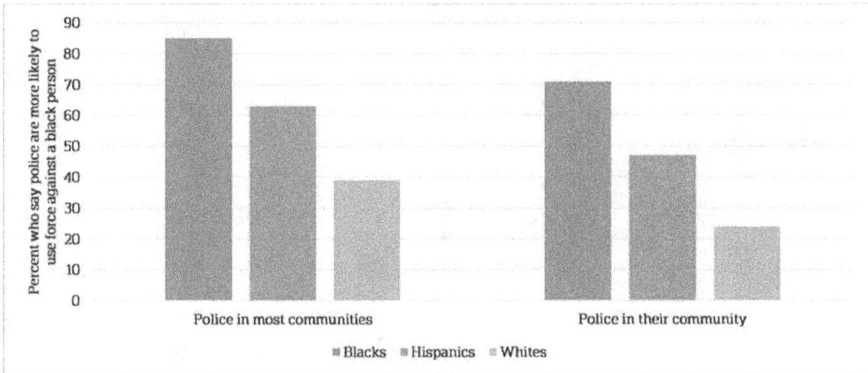

Questions: In general, do you think police in most communities are more likely to use deadly force against a black person, or more likely to use it against a white person, or don't you think race effects use of deadly force? What about your community? In general, do you think police in your community are more likely to use deadly force against a black person, or more likely to use it against a white person, or don't you think race effects use of deadly force?

Source: The Associated Press – NORC Center for Public Affairs Research (2015)

Specifically, regarding trust, it is reported that 60 percent of all

individuals who are American expressed trust in police locally, with

28 percent reporting that they trust their local police sometimes, and

11 percent reporting that they never trust their local police (The

Associated Press – NORC Center for Public Affairs Research,

2015). African Americans state that they rarely trust their local

police to "do what is best" (The Associated Press – NORC Center

for Public Affairs Research, 2015). The following chart shows the responses of African Americans, whites, and Hispanics to the question of the trust of their local police.

Figure 3
Whites are most likely to trust police to do what is right for them and their community

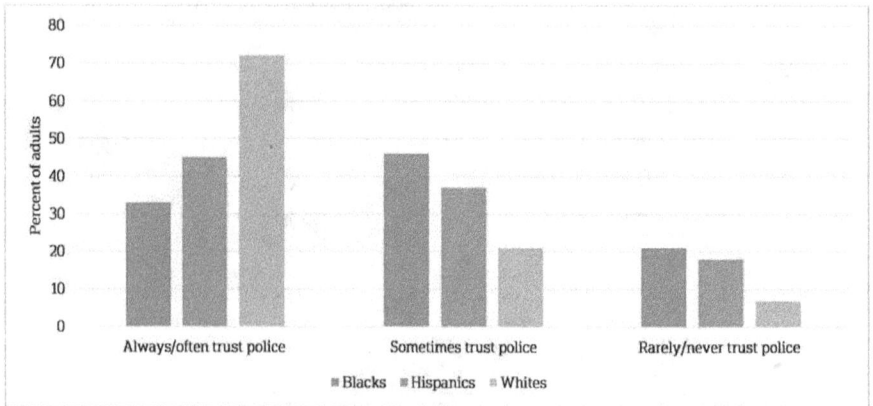

Question: How much of the time do you think you can trust the police to do what is right for you and your community?

Source: The Associated Press – NORC Center for Public Affairs Research (2015)

Fifty-four percent of American respondents in the study stated that police tend to treat individuals who are a minority in a rougher manner (The Associated Press – NORC Center for Public Affairs Research, 2015). Eighty-one percent of African Americans stated that police tend to treat individuals who are a minority in a rougher manner (The Associated Press – NORC Center for Public Affairs Research, 2015). It is reported that 70 percent of African Americans and 32 percent of whites believe that police officers receive lenient treatment more than they should (The Associated Press – NORC Center for Public Affairs Research, 2015). When encounters occur between civilians and police, it is reported that both fear violence (The Associated Press – NORC Center for Public Affairs Research, 2015). Community policing is listed as one intervention that the respondents in the study believe would be effective in bringing about reductions in police violence (The Associated Press – NORC Center for Public Affairs Research, 2015).

Pickett (2005) relates "Racial bias in our criminal justice system has many causes historical, political, and economic—but we know that any solution to the growing crisis of mass black incarceration must begin with focusing on how our communities, especially our youth are policed" (p. 74). Furthermore, Pickett (2005) states that the police officers are the criminal justice gatekeepers, and as such "discretionary decisions every day about who is likely to commit a crime and who should be targeted by the criminal justice system; about who should be stopped, questioned, searched, and arrested" (p. 74). Additionally, the training of police officers, along with their bias and prejudice, greatly influences their decisions about whom to stop and when (Pickett, 2005).

Pew Research Center Study

The work of Drake (2015) reports a Pew Research Center study and states that the survey found that on a consistent basis that whites, and African Americans have views that are quite different in relation to confidence in the police progress on racial equality. The Pew Research study report that only 32 percent of African Americans, compared to 48 percent of whites, expressed a belief that a great deal of progress has occurred since 1963 (Drake, 2015).

However, in a poll conducted just after the police shooting of a Black man in Ferguson, Missouri, in 2014, it was reported that 80 percent of African Americans believed that this incident highlighted issues of great importance concerning race, while 37 percent of those who were white expressed this same belief (Drake, 2015). It is reported that African American individuals expressed far less confidence than did their white counterparts in their local police in treating the two races in an equal manner (Drake, 2015). Fifty-seven percent of African Americans who responded to the poll stated that most police departments in the United States did an insufficient job of holding officers accountable when misconduct occurred, compared with 27 percent of whites (Drake, 2015).

In addition, 57 percent of African Americans stated that the performance of police is poor in their determination of the use of force situationally, while only 23 percent of their white counterparts expressed this view (Drake, 2015). Drake (2015) additionally states that the Pew Research Center study found that 76 percent of African Americans expressed that problems exist in the criminal justice system regarding race and law enforcement, while this view was expressed by only 33 percent of their white counterparts. Drake (2015) reports that only 22 percent of African Americans believed that police had the potential to gain trust among those served in the community, while nearly 50 percent of whites held that this was possible. This statistic is important for my research. Do African Americans in the church outreach program have any hope that trust can be built with police?

Further reported in the work of Drake (2015) is that there were low expectations on the part of African Americans that trust of police could improve, which was confirmed by 34 percent of African Americans and 43 percent of white individuals held that trust of police would either improve or worsen. Research is pointing to the need to develop trust between the African American community and police. On the other hand, some say the police are doing their job in high-crime neighborhoods that have high numbers of African Americans living there.

High-Crime Neighborhoods

La Vigne, Fontaine, and Dwivedi (2017) state that in some communities in the United States the trust of the public in police officers "is a critical ingredient in public safety," but that this trust among the public "is tenuous at best" (p. 1). Furthermore, those living in these communities characterized by a high level of crime as well as being in communities with large disadvantages and who are witness to a strong presence of police. Also, violence and incarceration rates are exceedingly high and are led to question the criminal justice system and its equity and effectiveness (La Vigne, Fontaine, & Dwivedi, 2017).

There are strategies used by police officers in such areas that are overly aggressive and are such that "target quality-of-life infractions and drug-, gun-, and gang-related violence in ways that undermine public confidence" (La Vigne, Fontaine, and Dwivedi, 2017, p. 1). La Vigne, Fontaine, and Dwivedi (2017) report a study on the community's perceptions of police officers in a high-crime and low-income community. The study reported that police could build trust in several ways in these communities including: (1) attempt to do the best thing for those with whom they are dealing.

(2) assist the population with those with whom they are dealing; (3) provide an explanation of their actions and decisions in a manner in which the public can easily understand; (4) have respect for the rights of the public; (5) provide the public with the opportunity to explain things from their position before proceeding; (6) treat the public with respect and dignity; (7) make law-based decisions

instead of decisions arising from personal beliefs or opinions; and (8) make decisions that are impartial and fair.

The views of police are found to be quite low in the areas of (1) police being authorities who are legitimate; (2) police and the public desiring things that are the same in their community; (3) police arrests are based on reasons that are good to believe that the individual has actually committed a crime; (4) police are sincere in assisting the public; (5) police possess the same idea of what is right and what is wrong as the public; (6) laws enforced by police are representative of the same values of the public; (7) police are supported for how they work in the community; (8) police arrest people for reasons that are not good; (9) police defend important values; (10) actions of police are consistent with the public's idea of what is right and what is wrong; and (11) when police are dealing with the public they behave in accordance with the law (La Vigne, Fontaine, & Dwivedi, 2017).

In the study, 55 percent of respondents stated they believed that they were treated with injustice upon the basis of their race (La Vigne, Fontaine, & Dwivedi, 2017). Interestingly, only 28 percent stated that their police department is responsive to community concerns (La Vigne, Fontaine, and Dwivedi, 2017, p. 10). When asked whether all laws should be obeyed, 74.3 percent stated yes (La Vigne, Fontaine, & Dwivedi, 2017, p. 11). About whether being law obedient resulted in community benefits, 72.9 percent stated yes (La Vigne, Fontaine, & Dwivedi, 2017, p. 11). It is interesting that only 54.2 percent stated that an individual who breaks laws are dangerous to the community (La Vigne, Fontaine, and Dwivedi, 2017, p. 11). Even lower, 49.2 percent believe that the laws in the United States are consistent with the community views concerning what is right and what is just (La Vigne, Fontaine, & Dwivedi, 2017, p. 11).

When questioned about how they can relate to police officers, only 42.9 percent of respondents in the study reported that they could "imagine being friends with a police officer" (La Vigne, Fontaine, & Dwivedi, 2017, p. 12). Even lower is the response of only 37.8 percent of respondents in the study who reported feeling safe around their police officers (La Vigne, Fontaine, & Dwivedi, 2017, p. 12). Only 36.3 percent of the respondents in the survey reported feeling comfortable around their police officers, and a mere

30.1 percent stated that they have trust in their police officers (La Vigne, Fontaine, & Dwivedi, 2017, p. 12). Those respondents who reported a belief that their police officers are honest was a mere 23.8 percent (La Vigne, Fontaine, & Dwivedi, 2017, p. 12).

In an *American Renaissance* report (2017) titled "The Color of Crime," it is reported that if there is indeed racial bias on the part of police in arrests made. Victim and witness surveys show that police arrest violent criminals in close proportion to the rates at which criminals of different races commit violent crimes. It is additionally reported that the differences in the rates of crimes among different races are dramatic and that the lowest rates of crime are among Asians, with the highest rates of crime among those who are African American (American Renaissance, 2017). For example, it is reported that in New York City, a city with a high crime rate, that an African American was twenty-one times more likely than a white person to be arrested for murder (American Renaissance, 2017, p. 1). The work of Weitzer and Tuch (2008) states that individuals who are of a minority ethnic or racial group many times believe that they are targeted for abuse by police officers. However, it is reported that when the factors shaping the attitudes of citizens toward police officers has as its starting point characteristics personal to the individual. Weitzer and Tuch (2008) state, however, that research has revealed that the area in which the individual lives plays an important role in how police officers view those living in these areas and affects the relations between citizens and the police. Furthermore, the work of Desmond, Papachristos, and Kirk (2016) says that citizens in Black communities often fail to report crimes because police officers are more likely to react violently to Black perpetrators of crime.

The above research points to the historical racial problems that have existed between the police and the African American community. Police have been the enforcers of segregated laws that have harmed African Americans physically, socially, emotionally, and economically. Distrust has become an appropriate response under these conditions. The church's outreach program will help build trust of reliability and respect. The next section of the literature will concentrate on interventions attempted to build trust.

Interventions

Interventions are purposive actions utilized to alter a behavior, reduce risk, or improve outcomes. Parenthetically, an intervention may reduce risk either by directly lowering vulnerability or by strengthening protective factors that buffer against risk (Fraser, Richman, & Galinsky, 2009, p. 9). Literature reveals different types of interventions utilized to build trust between the African American community and police.

Community Interventions

The work of Pickett (2005) sets out methods to reduce police violence against African Americans, including getting to know those police officers who are on patrol duty in the individual's neighborhood. Pickett (2005) relates that it is important for younger people to be counseled on their method of conducting themselves should they have a confrontation or be stopped by police officers. It is also recommended that the high schools send out invitations to police officers to visit the school and engage with students. Furthermore, elected officials and leaders locally should be held responsible for such incidents of police brutality and changes in policy (Pickett, 2005).

There are reported to be specific roles that community leaders and elected officials play that are community conscious and ensure that all police officers are professionally trained in the areas of cultural sensitivity, racial profiling, and policies on excessive force (Pickett, 2005). In addition, it is important that police departments be effective, diverse, and that there be the creation of mechanisms for oversight that are effective, as well as the elimination of any and all barriers to the filing of complaints by citizens (Pickett, 2005).

According to *The President's Task Force on 21st Century Policing Implementation Guide* (2015), there are five actions that government agencies can take in the area of community policing. The first action is creating the opportunity for listening to different groups and community areas. Second, there should be the provision of local government structure and other staff capabilities to support law enforcement reporting on activities related to the implementation of the task force recommendation. Procedures, policies, as well as other records were not made public to the community.

Third, there should be surveys completed in the community in relation to their attitudes about police and then the publication of the results. It is important that metrics and baselines be established so that progress can be measured, and the results used in community engagement and dialogue. Fourth, there should be an operational definition about the form of oversight by civilians to meet the community's needs. It is reported that in many cities there has been the establishment of citizen oversight that is independent in the form of a board that conducts a review of complaints relating to misconduct on the part of police officers.

Finally, action to effectively address crime should be taken by local governments that recognizes the correlation between socioeconomic conditions and the increase in crime, and then connect economic development with that of reduction of poverty and strategies for solving problems that are long term. There are reported to be five specific actions that law enforcement agencies can take to make provision of leadership and create an open climate as well as engaging members in the community according to *The President's Task Force on 21st Century Policing Implementation Guide* (2015). The first is to review and update policies as well as training and to conduct collection of data on police officer force that is used. There should be an emphasis on de-escalation as well as upon available alternatives to the arrest of citizens when it is appropriate. The second action is the increase of transparency through a collection of data and making the data accessible to the public.

The third action is the Peace Officer Standards and Training (POST) Commission to implement training at all levels to ensure fair and impartial policing. The fourth action is to conduct an examination of practices for hiring so that the community is more involved and engaged in the recruitment process and the screening process of applicants. The fifth action is to make sure that police officers can access the necessary tools needed to ensure their safety, including bulletproof vests and tactical training and first aid supplies.

Need for School Intervention

The work of Lurigio, Greenleaf, and Flexon (2009) reports that one of the variables that is of the greatest power in explaining the attitudes of the public toward police officers are that of race. Furthermore, the majority of studies in this area of inquiry have found that there is less satisfaction of the police among African American students than other races of the police. African Americans in Chicago had a higher likelihood than other races of students to experience police encounters (Lurigio, Greenleaf, & Flexon, 2009). Lurigio, Greenleaf, and Flexon (2009) additionally report that in previous studies the factors that resulted in trust for police was the police providing explanations for their actions that were honest to people, as well as giving consideration to other people's views when making decisions. In addition, it is conveyed in the work of Lurigio, Greenleaf, and Flexon (2009) that police were more trusted when people believe that their basic rights are being protected by the police.

Lurigio, Greenleaf, and Flexon (2009) report that another predictor of importance is that of age about the attitudes held by people toward police officers. It has been discovered in previous studies that people who are younger tend to have attitudes that are unfavorable for police officers and to have less confidence in police offers than older people do (Lurigio, Greenleaf, & Flexon, 2009). Lurigio, Greenleaf, and Flexon (2009) reported that the views of African American students and Latino students were different toward police in the area of three specific factors, including whether school commitment affected the view of students toward police officers. This involved a measure of the attitudes of students toward their teachers and school.

The hypothesis in the study reported by Lurigio, Greenleaf, and Flexon (2009) was "that students who had no contact with the police or who were treated respectfully during field contact would express more favorable views of the police," meaning that officers who demeaned youth during their interaction would not be trusted, but that receiving treatment that was fair students would hold views that were more favorable of police officers. Lurigio, Greenleaf, and Flexon (2009) report that 943 students were interviewed, and findings show that students who cared about their teachers' views of them reported they had more respect for police officers than students who did not care what the opinion of their teachers was of them.

Church as a Political and Social Activator

The work of Trader-Leigh (2008) reports that the "African American church has a long history of addressing the 'worldly' needs of the African American community" (p. 7). In fact, the role of the church in the areas of the struggle with oppression and being mistreated has created a great role for the African American church in its communities (Trader-Leigh, 2008). The life of the African American church being in the community is continuously shaped by the experiences of African Americans (Trader-Leigh, 2008). In addition, the economic and social disparities make a requirement that the African American church is "vigilant in confronting the nature of inequality in this country" (Trader-Leigh, 2008, p. 7).

The work of DeYoung (2011) reports that the African American church assisted in shaping the vision for the Civil Rights Movement outcome as evidenced in the statement of Dr. King: "It is true that as we struggle for freedom in America we will have to boycott at times. But we must remember that as we boycott that the boycott is not an end within itself... The end is reconciliation; the end is redemption; the end is the creation of the beloved community" (DeYoung, 2011, p .7). According to DeYoung (2011), "Justice, peace, and reconciliation remain central to the Black church today" (p. 7).

According to Black and Kari (2010), improving the lines of communication between the police and the community is the most important aspect relevant to improving the relations and rebuilding trust between the two groups. Studies have shown that public education and communication are vital elements in improving the race relations between African American citizens and the police force (Brunson & Weitzer, 2011). These studies have alluded to the fact that the lack of communication between the two groups has resulted in reluctance on both sides to begin the communication process to repair the broken relationship. Unfortunately, this is where the African American church may be failing its extended family members.

Cook (2013) points out that the role of church officials in the African American communities encompasses a great deal more than spiritual guidance. The church plays an active role in the political, social, and other issues that are relevant to the community, making the leaders more valuable in the eyes of their members. Davis (2012) conveys there is a sense of mystery around how and why African American ministers have so much influence over the lives of members of their congregations. However, on richly studying the African American culture and by understanding it, the question is effectively answered.

The answer goes back to the church being the center of everyday life and culture in the community. Spiritual leaders set examples of how the community perceives and reacts to different social issues, which validates the declaration that this is an excellent opportunity for the church. Especially the Church of Christ, as it stimulates the practice of leadership and active Christlike intervention in repairing the community's relationship with the police (Lowe & Shipp, 2014). However, ministers may have hidden agendas that result in self-promotion. Their theology of defiance may create more division than unity. It is imperative that ministers who seek unity become involved in bringing the police and the African American community together.

The question remains of how the church can help its members learn how to communicate with and trust the police. Young, Griffith, and Williams (2014) assert that pastoral counseling plays a vital part in the overall recovery process between church members and police. Pastoral counseling is essential, as it allows the understanding of Christ-like intervention to enter into the hearts of the members and to take center stage in the healing process.

Organized politically and spiritually, the African American church became fond of the teachings of Christianity. Furthermore, African American churches faithfully relied upon Christianity to deal with specific dilemmas that affected their people. African American Christians, regardless of their denominational distinctions, have relied upon the church to represent their religion, profession, and home.

The Role of the Police

Police officers have a significant responsibility in the community. Law enforcement is central to community safety. They can be observed giving a traffic ticket, making arrests, watching for criminal activity, and investigating a crime scene. The role of police in the community has typically been described to protect and serve, but the question with this motto is whether protecting and serving applies to all races in the community (Bain & Conser, 2014). As previously noted, police are looked upon and treated as a body of authority in a community. However, there have been officers who have abused their discretionary powers to the point where harm rather than good has been done to the community (Black & Kari, 2010). This type of ill-treatment has contributed to feelings of mistrust toward police in general within the African American community. This has spurred police to try to make positive steps toward correcting perceptions.

For starters, the concept of community policing was introduced into the American criminal justice system to give the community a more positive outlook about the police and give citizens a positive step in building relations with officers (Brunson, 2015). Community policing is a unique style of policing that involves the community and presents officers as partners in safety, not as aggressive authority figures that members of the community have to fear (Bain, Robinson, & Conser, 2014, August 12). Unfortunately, despite the efforts put into promoting the positive aspects of community policing, there are still officers who abuse their powers.

Lurigio, Greenleaf, and Flexon (2009) conducted a study that portrayed how interaction between police and African American youth were positive when working privately, one on one. A church's ministers can achieve these same results in a community. If this program has proven to be successful, a teaching program will be distributed among police departments as well as African American churches so that the same results can be achieved in those communities. Eventually, with Christ-like intervention being the focus that drives the current work, police relations and trust can be rebuilt with the African American church. MacDonald and Stokes (2006) suggest that by improving the trust between the two groups, social capital can be increased in the African American community.

The U.S. Department of Justice (2007) report titled "Building Trust Between the Police and the Citizens They Serve" reports that "Community trust is an established and highly honored relationship between the agency and the citizens it has been entrusted to serve" (p. 7). Trust existing between police and the community is critical to policing being effective (U.S. Department of Justice, 2007). The responsibility is borne by executives in law enforcement for the competence as well as the legitimacy and the integrity of their department (U.S. Department of Justice, 2007). If community trust is to be built, then police chiefs and those in management and supervision positions are responsible for fostering department environments where ethical behavior is to be expected and where individuals are responsible for aligning with those expectations (U.S. Department of Justice, 2007).

It is specifically stated by the U.S. Department of Justice (2007) that when the chiefs of police are clear about the processes of internal affairs in their department and recognize when misconduct has occurred and have addressed it appropriately, then the citizens who are in the jurisdictions will respond with confidence and respect for police officers. If community trust is to be constructed, then police departments must necessarily ensure adherence to integrity principles as well as professionalism because these are the foundations of building trust among members of the community (U.S. Department of Justice, 2007). Police officers hold a position of power that must be trusted in their community. Abuse of power can destroy trust and credibility.

Every individual police officer is representative of the whole agency (U.S. Department of Justice, 2007). However, internal affairs that are transparent are just one aspect of building trust in the community (U.S. Department of Justice, 2007). The culture of the agency should be one characterized by conduct that is ethical and integrity (U.S. Department of Justice, 2007). Where command staff properly supervises police officers, there will rarely be the need to make use of the function of internal affairs (U.S. Department of Justice, 2007).

It is reported that "Culture-changing policies, programs, and training are meaningful and effective not only in preventing misconduct and corruption in the department but also in demonstrating the agency's values and principles" (U.S. Department of Justice, 2007, p. 13). In addition, it is important that executives of police make sure that there is communication of the organization's core values and principles as well as these being both communicated and reinforced across the entire operations of the police department (U.S. Department of Justice, 2007). The principles and ethical standards should be set in writing in the form of a manual so that everyone has a clear understanding of the standards to which police officers are held (U.S. Department of Justice, 2007).

The recommended model by the U.S. Department of Justice is shown in the following figure.

Figure 4: Recommended Model

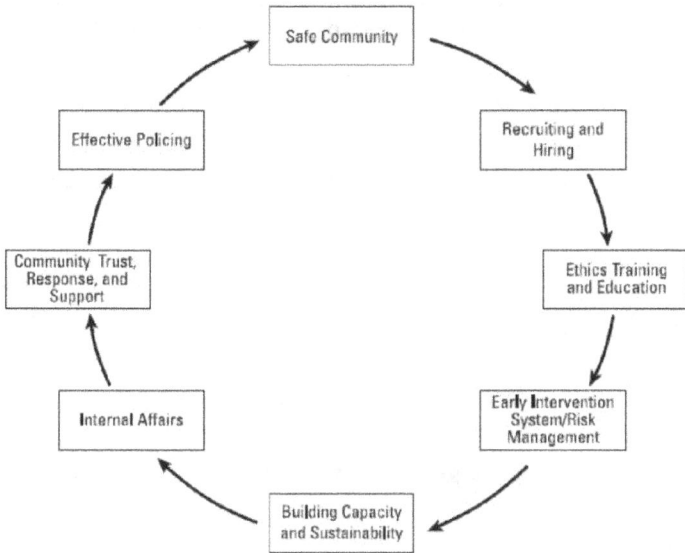

Source: U.S. Department of Justice (2007, p. 8)

Police and Ministers Collaboration

One example of police and African American pastors collaborating is in Boston, Massachusetts. In 1992, a group of Black activist clergy formed The Ten Point Coalition (TPC) after a gang assault on the Morningstar Baptist Church in Boston. Rival gang members of the deceased attacked grieving friends and family with guns and knives. Consequently, the TPC ministers felt a calling to help the community control gang activity and prevent youth from joining (Braga, 2003).

The ministers worked closely with the Boston Police to successfully create and implement the well-known Operation Cease Fire initiative. The goal of Operation Cease Fire, implemented in the mid-1990s, was to crack down on gang activities on the streets of Boston. The community, especially ministers, participated in varies ways to assist police in executing anti-violence operations and offer programs that would deter youth from crime (Braga, 2003).

Before Operation Cease Fire, the Boston Police and African American ministers were oppositional in how police were preventing crime, especially gang violence. The Boston Police were utilizing a "stop and frisk" method that angered the community. Pastors had concerns about the fragile relations between police and the community (Brunson, 2007). Operation Cease Fire placed church leaders on the frontline with the police. Pastors worked the community to gain information about gangs to share with the police.

Police shared information with ministers, and the two groups began to form working relationships to decrease gang violence in Boston. Individual relationships developed between police officers and ministers. However, the initiative had less influence on building trust between the two groups as a whole (Braga, 2003).

Methods of Counseling and Systems Theory

Operation Cease Fire and the Ten Point Coalition (TPC) working together can be classified as systems theory in action. The two groups working together became a stronger force than if they were functioning individually. The police became more effective with the ministers advocating and standing with them. Also, the ministers having the police as a resource gain power to enforce appropriate laws within the community. The success of these two organizations working together gives credence to the potential of the West Eastland Church of Christ outreach program.

The uniqueness of this research is that I am both a minister and a licensed marital and family therapist. I observed both the police and the African American community as two interacting systems.

The family systems theory perfectly fits here because of its emphasis on relating patterns. When pastors and ministers are delivering Christ-like intervention into the lives of its members, it is critical to establish the types of counseling methods utilized. According to Moore and Neiderhiser (2014), the most important element of the counseling process is to treat church members as family and use appropriate family therapeutic methods when entering into the counseling process.

Karakurt and Silver (2014) further explain that the family systems theory closely identifies and works well with family members who have experienced trauma and are trying to go through the healing process. Furthermore, the family systems model states that a client is apt to achieve better results seeking therapy in a family setting than individually, especially when the issue is centered on the family or group with which the patient identifies (Karakurt & Silver, 2014).

Combrinck-Graham (2014) furthers this theory as one that is extremely helpful in situations like the one described in this study because of the sense of family that is cultivated by the African

American church to its community members. Further, pastoral counseling conducted by the leaders of that community's church reinforces the ideas that are relevant to correct the fractured perception of the police by members of the community. BoydFranklin (2013) summarizes that the ability of the church officials to understand their clients' experience gives them a unique perspective in assimilating their problems and allows them to effectively help the client take a personal journey of changing their perception of the police. If the church community can accomplish changing their perception, it will give ministers a new sense of respect as well as a certain additional measure of influence within their community.

This study examined the work of three system theorists, including Bronfenbrenner, Minuchin, and Bozsurmenji-Nagy. The theorists in this study all hold that various aspects of the individual's world interact in different ways such as described in Bronfenbrenner's ecological systems theory and the contextual theory of Bozsurmenji Nagy, and finally the structural theory and systemic interactions related to the work of Minuchin. These three theories will demonstrate how the African American community and the police influence each other from a systemic perspective.

Uri Bronfenbrenner (1977) states that to understand human development, one must consider the entire ecological system in which growth occurs. Police and the church are two interfacing groups that interact with one another. The system, according to Bronfenbrenner (1977), is comprised of five socially organized subsystems that help support and guide human growth: (1) microsystems, (2) mesosystems, (3) exosystems, (4) chronosystems, and (5) macrosystems. The mesosystem would best define the interrelation between the police and the church collaborating for the benefit of the community. The community can profit from healthier teamwork between police and the church.

The mesosystem is reported in the work of Gauvin and Cole (1994) to formulate the links as well as the processes that are occurring in and between at least two settings in which the developing person is in, such as home-school and school workplace. Gauvin and Cole (1994) report that the chronosystem speaks of the passage of chronological time. The macrosystem is reported by Bronfenbrenner (1977) to be comprised of the

"overarching pattern of micro-, meso- and exo-systems characteristic of a given culture of subculture" (p. 515).

Bozsurmenji Nagy's theory, known as the "Contextual Theory" is relevant to explaining the ongoing trust issues that continue to exist between the police and the African American community. His theory concerns itself with fairness, loyalty, trust, and entitlements within families. All are relevant in establishing a better relationship between the police and the African American community. Nagy gave the name "multi-directed partiality" to the therapeutic technique of recognizing each person's view of the problem. He feels that when people find that they will be listened to in the session, they will be more willing to hear other members of the family. Thus, the multi-directed partiality begins the process of "rejunction" that he identifies as the goal of therapy (Boszormenyi-Nagy, 1997). According to contextual theory, police and the community can earn credits in the eyes of each other by doing something nice. The outreach program intentionally develops opportunities for the two groups to have positive interactions. Both credits and debts are transgenerational. The community and police are tied together for their existence and therefore must develop a working relationship.

Salvador Minuchin developed Structural Family Therapy and held that the rules of the family could be defined as being an invisible set of functional demands that persistently organizes family interactions (Minuchin, 1974). The interaction within the household must create trust. Minuchin's theory is relevant to this study because one objective of the outreach program is to develop trust between police and the church through planned interactions. Minuchin held that the family might be either functional or dysfunctional by the capacity of the family in their making adaptation to various stressors including those that are developmental, extrafamilial, and idiosyncratic (Minuchin, 1974). The planned interaction stressor was noted when some police were told by their superior to sit in seats where they could not all sit together. Uncomfortable boundaries can establish trust.

The subsystems of families are reported to have characteristics including a hierarchy of power, typically with the parental subsystem on top of the offspring subsystem (Minuchin, 1974). This model holds that the families that are healthy are those formed by boundaries between parents and children that are both clear and semi-diffuse, allowing parents to interact together with some degree of authority in negotiating between themselves and the methods and goals of parenting. However, families that are dysfunctional have subsystems that are mixed in nature as well as power hierarchies that are improper (Minuchin, 1974). The discretionary powers of the police can place them in an improper hierarchy.

Summary

The objective of this study is to evaluate a church outreach program which was developed to build trust between the police and a Black church following the death of Trayvon Martin. The church, community, law enforcement, and school play roles in addressing the issues relating to the unjustified use of police force against African Americans. The theoretical framework of this study was based on the systems theory and specifically the role of systems in developing trust. Therefore, this study examined the work of three system theorists, including Bronfenbrenner, Minuchin, and Bozsurmenji-Nagy. The theorists reviewed in this study all hold that various aspects of the individual's world interact in various ways such as described in Bronfenbrenner's ecological systems theory and the contextual theory of Bozsurmenji-Nagy, and finally the structural and systemic interactions related to the work of Minuchin.

As noted here, the neighborhoods and communities in primarily African American areas have changed since the 1990s, in that no longer is the community highly connected, and presently there is a climate of a police state in primarily African American communities. This literature has related how there is targeting of African American men and youth with police officer violence that is not justified and that there have been many wrongful charges and ultimately convictions of African American individuals who were later proved to be innocent.

This study reported that there is a general agreement among all racial groups that there needs to be procedural as well as policy changes to reduce violence of police officers against African American individuals. This study has, however, examined the ecological environment of this problem and has found that there are things that can be done by various groups within the environment to bring about positive changes in the levels of trust between police officers and the African American community. First, this study has found that leaders in the community elected officials to be culturally sensitive, aware of racial profiling, and receptive to mitigating this on the part of law enforcement officers and to addressing the use of unjustified and excessive force by police officers.

Trust can be built between law enforcement and African American communities through holding meetings, allowing. citizens to pose questions, and even enabling them to express their anger toward the police officers in their community. This study had additionally reported on the actions that the government agencies, police officers, and the community can take in establishing trust and better relations between police officers and those in the African American community.

Community policing has been found to be an efficient method for creating trust and reducing conflict in African American communities between the community and police officers. This effort can create an environment of collaboration between citizens and police officers and engage the public in activities that involve police officers, including fundraising events and volunteering. A higher level of training for police officers in coping with encounters with African American individuals is also vital to ensure that trust can be established. Engaging schools and churches in interactions with police officers can also be highly effective regarding creating a relationship of trust between law enforcement and those in the African American community.

Police officers can visit schools and churches to get to know people in them, as well as participate in community events and other forms of interaction other than law enforcement, which builds community trust in police officers. The African American church has always played a vital role in the African American community. Law enforcement collaboration and cooperation with the African American church enables law enforcement and the community to get to know one another. Also, findings of this study include that the everyday interactions of police officers and community members can be a trust-building opportunity. The next chapter of this study will discuss in detail the method used to evaluate the church's outreach program.

CHAPTER 3

RESEARCH METHODOLOGY

As previously stated, the current research was an evaluation of an African American church's outreach program to build trust with the local police. The purpose of the study was to explore the experiences and perceptions of African Americans and police about establishing trust through the church's outreach program. Trust between the two parties has not been fully explored in Gallatin, Tennessee. As will be discussed, a qualitative study is the appropriate research methodology for this learning.

To achieve the purpose, the following research questions were a guide to evaluate effectiveness of the church's outreach program designed to build trust between the Gallatin police and the West Eastland Church of Christ located in Gallatin, Tennessee:

1. How has the outreach program of this church help-built trust with the police department?

2. What was the role of this church in helping the outreach program build trust?

3. What was the role of the police department in helping the outreach program build trust?

4. How did the ecological systems theory (collaboration) assist in helping the outreach program build trust?

In this chapter, the details of implementing a qualitative research action project will be presented. The other sections of the chapter include: (a) population and sample, (b) procedures for data collection, (c) data analysis plan, and (d) ethical procedures.

Methodology and Research Design

Choosing the correct research method is an essential variable when conducting research. The adequacy of the study depends on the method and design being applied. The research design provides the overall structure for the procedure the researcher follows, the data the researcher collects, and the data analysis the researcher conducts (Leedy & Ormrod, 2016, p. 74). I ensured that I utilized the best and adequate research methods and design so that my study could be directed most appropriately. Furthermore, it is essential for the selection to be accurate to guarantee correct research on the designated topic. Methodology and design should not be selected based upon comfortableness but upon what will yield the best results.

Research Methodology

There are three options when choosing a research methodology: quantitative, qualitative, and mixed methods. Quantitative methodology is appropriate for studies that involve the identification of possible significant relationships between two or more variables, which can be independent, dependent, or controlled (Mertens, 2014). Therefore, because quantitative research is essentially about collecting numerical data to explain a particular phenomenon, particular questions seem immediately suited to being answered using quantitative methods. The method of measurement is important to quantitative research because it affords the central construction between empirical observation and mathematical expression of quantitative relationships (Muijs, 2004, p. 2).

The mixed method is used when the research question has both a qualitative and quantitative component to address the problem of the study adequately. Some problems need both quantitative and qualitative data. The research involves not only collecting, analyzing, and interpreting both quantitative and qualitative research but also integrating conclusion from those data into a cohesive whole (Leedy & Ormrod, 2016, p. 311). If the study requires measurement and statistical analysis, a quantitative method provides the better choice. However, the purpose of this current research does not align with the description of the quantitative methodology and mixed method research. Therefore, a qualitative methodology was the best approach to apply in this study.

Qualitative methodology is used when the purpose of the research is to explore, investigate, explain, or describe a phenomenon within an uncontrolled environment, using data about perceptions, experiences, and behaviors of individuals (SavinBaden & Major, 2013; Silverman, 2016). A qualitative research approach was used to evaluate the church's outreach program. A phenomenological study utilizing two focus groups were used to gather perceptions and perspectives. This phenomenological study was used to understand and gather information about the church's outreach program experiences from police and church members' point of views (Leedy & Ormrod, 2016, p. 255, 258). The information collected helped me critique strengths, weaknesses, threats, and opportunities of the outreach program.

The goal of qualitative research is to deeply explore a specific phenomenon or experience on which to build further knowledge or to develop a more focused practice that is sensitive to the research participants (Savin-Baden & Major, 2013). Moreover, a qualitative study provides an opportunity to understand a phenomenon as it relates to the meaning other people derive from the experience or situation (Silverman, 2016). The aspect of interest for this study was to evaluate how well the church's outreach program is building trust between police and the West Eastland Church of Christ.

Role of the Researcher

A qualitative research interviewer can influence collected data. The qualitative researcher's role is familiar to me as a licensed marital and family therapist and as a Clinical Fellow with the American Association of Marriage and Family Therapy. A Clinical Fellow is known for rigorous training in marriage and family therapy and competent skills recognized around the world. My years as a counselor enhance my skills to ask follow-up open-ended questions and correctly interpret nonverbal communication of participants. The interaction between the therapist and his client resembles the interviewer's interaction with research participants.

Buetow (2013) discusses four roles of the qualitative researcher. First, the interviewer as a traveler is a socially situated encounter with the informant. The interviewer and informant construct and share their understandings. Second, the interviewer as a miner focuses on uncovering waiting nuggets of social reality. These nuggets are assumed to exist objectively and independently of the informant. However, they are accessible only through the informant's representations of them by conscious experience.

Third, the interviewer as a cleaner resembles the miner but goes further by seeking to cleanse, as far as possible, the interview questions from bias. Fourth, the interviewer as a conductor is a reflective and interpretive practitioner. The conductor experiences and binds together a "force field" that can create order from the different interviewing roles of the traveler, miner, and cleaner. Across and even within individual interviews, the conductor integrates these beliefs to drive or restrain transitions between, or a blurring, of these roles. My role in this research resembles more of a conductor's, utilizing the roles of the traveler, miner, and cleaner.

Research Design

A qualitative research design utilizing a focus group will be used to evaluate this program. Focus groups provide insights into how people think and provide a deeper understanding of the trust issues between the two groups. The group is focused on the sense that it involves some collective action and is dissimilar from the broader category of group interview by the explicit use of the group interaction as research data (Kitzinger, 1994). Good interviewing skills are needed to conduct a focus group. My background as a licensed marital and family therapist fits with the focus group approach. Focus groups provide an opportunity to hear participants and observe body language. I observed how the participants interacted and reacted to one another. It is also less time consuming and less expensive. However, some drawbacks to focus groups are its deficiency of anonymity and lack of participation by some. The interviewer may misinterpret nonverbal of participants and inadvertently influence collected data (Kuhn, 2000), and interviewer biases can influence the outcome of the study if left unaddressed (Sorsa, Kiikkala, Astedt-Kurki, 2015).

Population and Sample

The target population for this study was composed of two focus groups: Caucasian police officers and African American members of a local church in Gallatin, Tennessee. The target population was extremely specific in order to be aligned with the specific problem of the study. The target population was based on the requirements of the purpose, which involves exploring trust issues and experiences of police officers and African American members of a local church in Gallatin, Tennessee. The intent of a qualitative study is not to generalize a population, but to develop an in-depth exploration of a central phenomenon. To best understand the phenomenon, qualitative researchers intentionally select individuals and sites. Therefore, focusing on these individuals who have the necessary characteristics to provide the information that is needed to address the problem will be useful in answering the research questions of the study.

From the population, a sample was be selected. Researchers showed that the sample size for qualitative research is based on data saturation, which is a point in the data collection when only an insignificant amount of new information is added to existing data with the addition of one more participant to the study (Fusch & Ness, 2015). Research shows that qualitative research requires about six to twenty participants to achieve data saturation (Fusch & Ness, 2015; Silverman, 2016). Since there are two groups to be explored, eight to ten participants were from the police in Gallatin, Tennessee, while another set of eight to ten participants from the African American members of a West Eastland Church of Christ, which is also in Gallatin, Tennessee.

Participants were recruited using purposive sampling, which is the most common technique used for selecting participants in qualitative studies (Barratt et al., 2015). Purposive sampling is a recruitment technique that uses targeted selection of individuals who are fit to address the research questions of the study based on a set of eligibility or inclusion criteria (Barratt et al., 2015; Etikan, Musa, & Alkassim, 2016). Researchers stated that participants recruited through purposive sampling tend to provide detailed information about the topic of a study because of their familiarity with the phenomenon of interest in the study (Barratt et al., 2015). Through this technique, the researcher is able to select participants with the relevant knowledge and experiences pertaining to the topic of the study (Barratt et al., 2015).

To begin the recruitment process, I got permission from church leadership and the chief of police to conduct the evaluation. Two groups were solicited for participation. These groups were held separately. Individuals for the focus group were solicited by invitational letters (see Appendix A) that were mailed to the police station and the church. The police captain distributed the letter to all that meet the criteria, and the elders did the same at the church. One group was officers from the police, and one group was members of the church. Each group consisted of eight to ten members, and sessions lasted for approximately ninety minutes. The interviews toke place at the local library or hotel conference room. Two or more groups were recommended, with focus groups, and small sample sizes are legitimate in qualitative research (Carlsen & Glenton,

2011). Individuals who could provide the best information were asked to participate. Due to this being a small police department, the goal was to have any officer participate who was not in a supervisory position. It is worth noting that officers had not spent the same amount time involved in the program; however, information could still be gained on how to improve the program.

In the invitation, I included the purpose and significance of the study to the community. I also included the scope for data collection. Those who agree to participate were asked to read and sign an informed consent form (see Appendix B), which I attached to the invitation. The informed consent form was also included in the information about the risks and scope of participation in the study. I visited the police station one week after distributing the invitations to collect signed informed consents. For church members, I collected the signed informed consent forms at the next scheduled church service. After receiving the signed informed consent, I discussed with the participant to confirm their eligibility. I also asked the participants for their preferred time and date for the interview.

Procedures for Data Collection

Two focused methods were used to gather data. At the date of the scheduled interview, I arrived at the location thirty minutes before the scheduled time to organize the materials needed: (a) interview questions, (b) audio recorder, and (c) writing materials.

I chose a location that was comfortable to the recipients as to create a friendly atmosphere. Each focus group was expected to last for about ninety minutes. I audio-record each session for purposes of transcription, subject to the approval of the participant, as stated in the informed consent.

When the participant arrived, I greeted and welcomed him or her. Refreshments were provided for participants. After refreshments and brief interaction, I then began with the introduction phase of the interview session. I briefly discussed the background of the study and the flow of the interview session to manage the expectations of the group. The main data source for this study was semi-structured open-ended interview questions (see Appendix B) that were asked of the groups. After the introduction phase, I begin asking questions to the group, starting with broad to a more specific question format. For every answer that a participant provides, I asked relevant follow-up questions to explore deeper into the answers given. After all the questions have been asked, participants were then allowed to ask any questions or verbalize any concerns. I acknowledged, determined, and addressed the concerns of the participants. After addressing each question or concern, I thanked the participants for taking time to be part of the study and offered a debriefing.

Data Analysis Plan

As part of the preparation of the data from the focus groups, I transcribed interviews for each group. After transcribing each interview, I wrote a one-page summary and interpretation of the data from the interviews. I then organized the soft copies of the transcripts and load them to the NVivo software, which is the tool that was used as an aid in analyzing the transcripts.

Thematic Analysis

The specific method for analyzing the data for this study was the six-step thematic analysis of Braun and Clarke (2014). Thematic analysis is the most common form of analysis in qualitative research.

Thematic analysis is where subthemes are identified from the data and linked with the research questions of the study. The subthemes will be derived from the results of the study. The six steps include: (a) familiarizing of data, (b) coding, (c) thematizing, (d) revising themes, (e) finalizing and defining themes, and (f) writing up (Braun & Clarke, 2014).

With my expertise in the subject, I was the analyst for the study. I began the analysis procedure by reading and rereading the transcripts to determine and identify potential points of analytical interest for the study. The data from the police and church groups were used to answer or address the research questions. From my notes, I identified key descriptive phrases that were relevant to addressing the research questions. I then coded the data set. The analysis continued with the grouping of similar codes and forming larger themes. I then identified larger patterns from the data coded before revising themes and developing a thematic map that helped in the identification of relationships between the themes.

As final procedures, I engaged in detailed analysis of the data in each theme to refine categories and their organization and completed a final refinement of the analysis that establishes its significance and contextualizes it in terms of existing theory and research. In the process, data was analyzed both inside each case and across cases. During the final phases of the analysis, I focused on different, contrasting perceptions. Data analysis also included triangulation between the three sources of data, leading to increased credibility and analysis validity (Yin, 2014), with the analysis noting whether a given theme emerges in one source, or similar or contradicting in multiple data sources.

The Validity of Data

For qualitative studies, the researcher has to ensure trustworthiness, which means ensuring that the study has credibility, dependability, and transferability based on the data collected, and the overall output of the study (Houghton, Casey, Shaw & Murphy, 2013; Lincoln & Guba, 1985). I will maintain the highest standard of ethics to ensure this research maintain trustworthiness. This will include accurate documentation of the experiences and voices of both focus groups.

Credibility

Credibility refers to the extent of truth in the data for a research (e.g., the answers of the participants to the interview questions) against how a researcher represents and interprets information during the analysis and discussion (Cope, 2014.

Lincoln & Guba, 1985). The qualitative aspect of this promoted credibility by acknowledging that the individuals or participants who provided the raw data collected from human experiences were people who share the same experiences (Cope, 2014). Moreover, using NVivo software helped me in the analysis, especially coding and thematizing the interview data and audio recordings. Therefore, there will be minimal human intervention or human error. Performing this step is a way to increase the accuracy of the study's findings. One of the advantages of using the NVivo software is that it can analyze the qualitative information gathered from the interviews directly from the audio recordings—that is, without that use of the interview transcripts. To ensure credibility,

I reviewed the transcripts and expert reviews of the instrument for the study (Fusch & Ness, 2015).

Transferability

Transferability is based on the orderly and thorough explanation of conclusions and insights that can be useful to other settings and related research (Cope, 2014). To address issues of transferability, I provided a complete description and variation in participant selection and results. Therefore, transferability may be improved by reviewing the text-based descriptions collected from the participants. Through the review, I made sure that the description and discussion of the implementation of the methodology of the study was exhaustive, deep, and rich (Miles, Huberman, & Saldana, 2014). By performing this, I could expect that output for the study can be useful to other research of other studies. I provided the complete and detailed description of the processes included in implementing the methodology of the study. Therefore, future researchers will be able to replicate the study to other populations.

Dependability

Dependability refers to data consistency for a study. To improve the dependability of the data, I provided a trail to complete documentation of the data relevant to implementing the methodology for this study. An audit trail is the compilation of relevant and tangible articles that can help to improve the accuracy and dependability of the data for the benefit of future researchers (Cope, 2014). Through the use of an audit trail, information can be gathered that serves as a second opinion of the processes and products of the study (Cope, 2014; Lincoln & Guba, 1985).

Confirmability

Human objectivity is based on the individual skills and perceptions (Cope, 2014). To improve confirmability, I made sure that the interview protocol had the same questioning. By providing identical questioning for both groups, I could make sure the information from the participants was cohesive and unified. In this way, the materials gathered would be considered authentic and can improve the confirmability of the data. Moreover, I aimed to improve the confirmability of the results by identifying any personal biases so that other people can evaluate the objectivity of the analysis (Miles et al., 2014). A possible personal bias to this study is my being an African American male.

Ethical Procedures

When using human subjects for a study, a researcher has the responsibility to address ethical issues. For this study I provided a discussion of how to protect the participants, based on the prescriptions of the University Institutional Review Board (IRB). I have gained permission from the IRB to collect data for this study.

Informed Consent

To make sure that ethical issues are addressed and made known to the participants, I have asked each respondent to read and sign an informed consent form (see Appendix B). Only the people who have read and agreed with the contents of the form signed the form and participate in the study. By signing the informed consent, the participants signify that they understand and agree with the information included in the form. In the consent form, I informed participants about potential risks, purpose of the study, participation scope, and individual rights as participants.

However, it was explained to participants that they could leave the group at any time. This qualitative research may provoke distressing emotions due to the historical and recent conflicts between the police and the African American community. Participants could stop and leave the interview at any time. Moreover, the risks or re-traumatization or psychological implications to the participants were minimal. Physical risks (e.g., injury, violent environment, etc.) were also minimal. Also included in the informed consent were the details of the scope of participation and the length of participating in the study. Storage procedures for the data and confidentiality issues was also discussed in the informed consent. Debriefings were offered after research is conducted.

Confidentiality

Another ethical issue to be addressed was confidentiality. I kept the identity of each participant confidential. No names, addresses, or telephone numbers were used that can be linked to participants. I used numbers to replace the names of the participants and any identifiable information about the participants. I was the only one who knew the identity of the participants and their corresponding pseudonyms. The numbers are used in all data files and reports for the study.

Voluntary Participation

I did not force any person (e.g., police officer or African American member of the local church) to be part of the sample for the study. There were no consequences for refusing to accept the invitation to participate. On the other hand, I did not give any incentives to those who accepted the invitation and took part in the study. Also, even after signing the informed consent, the participants were still allowed to quit the study. If there is an intention to terminate participation, the participant would need to inform me about the decision to no longer be a participant. The participant could inform me, either through email or printed letter, about this decision. Any information collected before the termination of participation was deleted or returned to the participant.

Limitations/Delimitations of Study

The first limitation of this study has to do with the size of the town, police department, and church. Gallatin, Tennessee, is a suburban city of Nashville with a population of 30,000 people. The city has twenty-six police officers, and the church has 150 members. Second, there was no consideration for gender and only race consideration from the church. Delimitations that I imposed upon the study were African American members from the predominately African American church and no one from the leadership team of the police. There is a need for further research from a metropolitan city with a more extensive police department and a church with more congregants. Furthermore, it would enhance this research to unearth how police of different races and gender view trust.

Summary

The purpose of this study was evaluating the West Eastland Church of Christ's outreach program designed to develop trust between the local police and the church. I used a qualitative study as the appropriate research methodology for this study. Qualitative research design proposes a valuable foundation for scientific inquiry when the experience is the focus of the study. The phenomenological method is particularly useful in bringing to light the full opportunity of experiences and perceptions from an individual's viewpoint. Two focused groups were used to gather data: Caucasian police officers and African American members of a local church in Gallatin, Tennessee. Eight to ten individuals were chosen for each group. I collected data from the groups. Data was analyzed using six-step thematic analysis. Within the identified limitations of the section, all ethical considerations were taken into account to ensure that all study participants can share their experience with the nominal risk of harm. The next chapter will discuss information and analysis from collected data.

CHAPTER 4

DATA ANYLYSIS

Chapter four of the study contains the analysis of the two focus group data with the church and police members. The purpose of this study was to evaluate an outreach program developed by an African American church to develop trust with the local police. Two focus group discussions were conducted, with the first group composed of church members and the second group composed of police. A qualitative thematic analysis was then performed to analyze the focus group data and search for the most common but meaningful patterns from the responses of the participants. NVivo 11 software by QSR was also employed to assist in the coding and tabulation of the responses to themes, and the order of significance of these themes was also developed with the help of the software. The major questions used to drive the discussions are as follows:

1. How has the outreach program of this church helped build trust with the police department?

2. What is the role of this church in helping the outreach program build trust?

3. What is the role of the police department in helping the outreach program build trust?

4. How does the ecological systems theory (collaboration) assist in helping the outreach program build trust?

The chapter also contains the demographics of the focus group discussion (FGD) participants, a review of the data analysis method, the presentation of findings discussing the generated themes supported by the verbatim responses from the FGDs, and a short summary to conclude the chapter.

Demographics

Two sets of participants were recruited for the study. The focus group discussions were conducted separately, with the first group being the African American members of the West Eastland Church of Christ, and the second group composed of Caucasian police officers. Both groups are from Gallatin, Tennessee. Each group session lasted ninety minutes. The church group consisted of nine individuals, and the police group consisted of six. Members for both groups were chosen based upon stated criteria in this research. Members of each group were given numbers randomly to ensure confidentiality while speaking into the recorder. These participants were recruited because they have firsthand perceptions and experiences of the outreach program and its ability to build trust. These participants shared and were open to new ideas emerging when discussing the subject at hand.

Data Analysis

The focus group data were analyzed using the six-step thematic analysis by Braun and Clarke (2014). The six steps were carefully and consistently followed to ensure the maximization of the data gathered and report them through the current research study. The thematic analysis allowed me to explore the data and identify the most important perceptions shared by the participants, interpret them strictly based on how the participants shared them, and report thereafter. The complete coding table containing the themes and the participant responses is found in Appendix C. The themes with the greatest number of references were considered as the *major themes* of the study, per research question and group. The themes with fewer references following the major themes were tagged as the *minor themes*, and these themes are also the other most significant perceptions shared. Finally, *subthemes* were also incorporated to better detail and explain the major and minor themes.

Presentation of Findings

Each group was asked to define trust. From the interview conducted, trust, according to the church, is a way of demonstrating dependability and reliability with another person and believing that someone has your best interest and will do you no harm. Also, it means being relaxed and free that what you share with a person is kept in confidence. According to the police, trust refers to the ability to believe that when a person is assigned to do a task on behalf of another person, the trusted person will carry out the activity ethically without the other person being concerned about being hurt. The police emphasize that trust is not only telling someone confidential information, but it also means asking someone to do something and knowing that this person will accomplish the request without fail.

Building Trust Through the Outreach Program

The first research question asked how the outreach programs of the church help build trust with the police department. Data from the focus group discussions of the church members and police members were thematically analyzed. Each set had two major themes and several other minor and subthemes. Most church members discussed how the outreach program allowed the familiarization of community members with the police department. The following changes or improvements were observed: having the opportunity to communicate openly with the officers, seeing the officers as normal human beings, continuing the presence and visibility of the police members, and seeing the police members as community models.

Meanwhile, the police officials observed a similar change through the outreach program, which was also the familiarization of the two parties. This was in terms of having the opportunity to interact and communicate closely with the community members, modifying the image and perceptions of police officers, and seeing the officers as normal human beings. Table One contains the breakdown of the themes for both focus groups, answering the first research question of the study.

Table One

Breakdown of the Themes Answering Research Question One

Focus Group	Themes	Number of References
FGD One: Church Members	Familiarizing of community members with the police department *Having the opportunity to communicate openly with the officers *Seeing the officers as normal human beings *Continuing the presence and visibility of the police members *Seeing the police members as community models*	9
FGD Two: Police Officers	Familiarizing of community members with the police department *Having the opportunity to interact and communicate closely with the community members *Modifying the image and perceptions of police officers *Seeing the officers as normal human beings*	6
	Needing to remove the negative link between the police and racism *Opening of dialogues and conversations between the police and the community members*	1

*Note: Subthemes

Major Theme One: Familiarizing Community Members with the Police Department

The first major theme of the study was the familiarization of community members with the police department. Members of the church shared during the FGD how trust between the church and police members improved with the help of the outreach program. More specifically, the major theme was strengthened by four significant factors: having the opportunity to communicate openly with the officers, seeing the officers as normal human beings, continuing the presence and visibility of the police members, and seeing the police members as community models.

Each subtheme will be discussed further below.

Subtheme One: Having the opportunity to communicate openly with the officers

The first subtheme that built the trust of the community members with the police officials was the opportunity to communicate and interact openly through the program. During the FGD, the church members shared how the outreach program allowed the community members to be more comfortable around the police officers because of the increased interactions and conversations with the police officers. Participant One explained how the outreach program brought awareness to the community members that the police officers are just like any other human being. Despite their positions and profession, they are also approachable and are able to communicate with the civilians. The participant shared an example of how the outreach program changed the initial perceptions of the community members of the police officers:

> I believe that there is an awareness now that was not before, and that awareness brings comfort, and hope between the police and us. I know one day I was at the Paraclete Center delivering the bread, and just kind of there by myself, putting bread in bags and stuff like that. And the police officer drove up because he saw my car there, and immediately, I was like, "Oh no, I'm in trouble. What did I do? I'm just here." He walks up, and he is totally calm. There's nothing alarming about his presence. He just kind of knocks on the door. Of course, I got the door locked because it's nighttime, and I'm, like, you know, it's whatever.

But he walks up, and he's like, "Hey, what's up? What's going on?" You know, just asked the question. I'm fine, just doing this bread thing. And he was like, okay, and walks away. Like, there's no distrust there, nothing to, I mean, he was just checking it out. And I didn't feel like he was being threatening or that he was going to do anything crazy. And I think that was a misconception that has been built because of all this media frenzy and then the things that have been happening. So, it really put me at ease to know that they are not going to jump to conclusions first because they know what we are about here. And they recognize we are not a threatening presence and they do not want to be a threatening presence either (PA I).

Participant Two shared another example of how a simple conversation or interaction with a police officer can improve and change the perception of the civilians toward the police members. One encounter allowed for the participant to see the approachable and sociable side of police officers:

I can give an example of something that happened just recently. We had the alarm go off a couple of weeks ago, and an officer responded. And he came down here and he probably spent twenty to thirty minutes with us, just talking. He stood right there, and we talked, and he seemed to be very relaxed. He seemed to extremely comfortable in talking with us and smiling. I think he was laughing. So that to me showed that he was not in a rush to get away from us. He didn't feel threatened by us. It seemed to feel like... It seemed like he was not concerned that we were going to say something or report something on him maybe that wasn't true.

So, I have been around other situations where an officer is very official. You know, "What is wrong? Okay, you okay? See you later." But he was not like that. He spent time communicating with us. And as far as I know, none of us knew him by name or had met him before to say, this is officer so and so (PA II).

Meanwhile, Participant Four simply echoed the other participants' perceptions: "I think by them being an example, showing that they trust others, and then they communicate openly" (PA IV). Additionally, Participant Five stated how the programs allow the community and police members to interact and get to know another: By having the programs where they can come out and we collaborate, and they come out and speak, and just getting to know each other in those activities help. You know, kind of do an introduction and break down and make an attempt at building a relationship (PA V).

Participant Ten shared another interaction that allowed for the realization of the police members' openness and willingness to assist the community members in whatever way they can. The outreach program had the same effect on Participant Ten. He expressed how the program developed relationships further: I know the chief told me one time, I introduced myself when I got a new job and I happened to be working some of his relatives, and he said, yeah, I know so-and-so. So, he said, and he took, reached into his pocket, took out a card, and he said, "If you need anything, you call me." He put himself out there, so I feel that I can pick up the phone and call him if I needed him. So, I think that the outreach... I guess to me the key to all of it is building a relationship. If I do not know you and I haven't spent any time with you, why do I have any reason to trust you or rely on you? And I think that this spending time together and each side seeing that the other side is going to keep its word it is building trust (PA X).

Participant Eleven believed the outreach program altered the beliefs and views of the community about the police officers and the institution as a whole: "I believe that it's built trust by interacting with us, collaborating with us. It has dispelled some preconceived ideas that were maybe held about African Americans in this community" (PA XI). Finally, Participant Thirteen highlighted the importance of familiarizing oneself with the officials or officers:

Since you brought it up, like they come over to the closet over here, especially the new people. Everybody, I look, face that I do not see before, I ask, how do you know about us? You would be surprised. All of them put it out there on Facebook. They are getting it off Facebook. And that is what they tell me because if I do not know your face, I am going to ask you if it's your first time (PA XIII).

Subtheme Two: Seeing the officers as normal human beings

The second subtheme of the study was seeing the officers as normal human beings. This was a result of the constant communication and interaction between the community members and officers. Participant Three explained how the presence of the officials during the outreach programs and activities make the officials seem more normal and human in the eyes of the civilians, saying:

> I see it a little differently in terms of what we, all the numbers have said something that is extremely critical from the eyes of African Americans. I see it in the way that what we are doing through this outreach initiative is also what is known as "people first movements." And really what that means is that you do not see a title, you see the person first. So, we see people who are in uniforms. I think that police officers are people. Law enforcement are people who wear a uniform of authority. But when you can identify first with

the person and make that real to everyone, I think that that's really bridging the way to open communication and strengthening relationships (PA III).

Subtheme Three: Continuing the presence and visibility of the police members

The third subtheme was the positive influence of the constant presence and visibility of the police members. For Participant Eight, trust is built with a continuing presence and existence of the police officials within the community. This is one effect of the outreach program to the community members: I believe the trust building is also coming from just a continuance, a continuing presence in the neighborhood, and it is positive. And anytime you continue doing something, it just builds and builds. So, the trust building is a level, a step-by-step process (PA VIII).

Subtheme Four: Seeing the police members as community models

The final subtheme reported how the program allowed police members to be viewed as community role models. Participant Four stated the outreach program gives the policemen the opportunity to show a more positive look of their lives: "I think by them being an example, showing that they trust others, and then they communicate openly" (PA IV).

From the analysis of the second focus group, another major theme was discovered. The same theme was shared by the police members, where the church's outreach program led to the familiarization of community members with the police department. Another minor theme with fewer references was discovered that revealed the need to remove the negative link between the police and racism. However, the minor theme is only found in the Table One, as the theme may need further research for validity.

Major Theme Two: Familiarizing Community Members with the Police Department

The second major theme was the familiarization of community members with the police department. Three factors were identified: having the opportunity to interact and communicate closely with the community members, modifying the image and perceptions of police officers, and seeing the officers as normal human beings. Through these themes, it can be seen how the constant collaboration and association improved the perception of the church members or civilians by the police officials or members.

Subtheme One: Having the opportunity to interact and communicate closely with the community members

The first subtheme was the opportunity to interact and communicate closely with community members. Three of the police officers shared during the group that constant networking and conversations with the community result in better relationships and increased trust. One participant shared how a church activity helped civilians realize the willingness of police officers to help and assist the community. Additionally, the participant's openness and genuine care for the community members allowed for the initial misconceptions and negative behaviors of the civilians to be altered as well:

> I will say, you know, two or three years ago when we entered into our relationship with the church, I asked you all if we could do our National Night Out Against Crime at your church, and backpack giveaways and things like that at the church. I will say that that did help, and I will give a prime example of what... I had to take a response. In the day that we were giving backpacks out, it was kind of unusual, I had

to take a complaint from a female, African American female, that came up and complained about an officer.

And she, I mean, she let me have it. She told me that I, you know, I did not care about the community, I did not care about the African community. And, you know, I took her complaint. I was as nice as I possibly could be to her. Then, that night we had come over to the church, and we are handing out backpacks and hot dogs and coats, and she's in line with her daughter. Everybody was in line. She got the backpacks, and I was wrapping the hot dogs. And I leaned down and gave her daughter a hot dog and pulled a Coke out of the, you know, water and gave it to her, and I grabbed one and gave it to her. And, you know, she had to look me in the eye at that point, and she shook my hand. And she didn't say anything, but she shook my hand, and I could tell she was humbled at that point (PA Unidentified). Another participant explained how constant interactions allow the communication lines between the church/community members and the police officials to open. The participant also shared how the program allowed for a more comfortable setting for the two parties to get to know one another and remove the initial distrust and discomfort the civilians have toward the police officers:

> What I was talking about, we need to reach back in, is just what you said, open those lines of communication, let them see us, let them ask questions. If you do not understand, instead of being angry about it, let's ask the questions, whether it be through a reach-out group like you or... The door is always open. I would be happy to sit down with anybody in the community. And like Number Five said, we have to listen. We cannot just sit and have a conversation; we have to listen. They have to listen to us; we have to listen to them. No matter who that is in the community when I say "they," the people of the community have to listen. And that is why I say we can improve, is our dialogue (PA Unidentified).

Meanwhile, a male participant added how the outreach program allow them to communicate and speak with a larger group of people outside the usual setting or negative environment when the civilians encounter them on duty. The participant believed a lighter setting allows for both parties to be their true selves and communicate more effectively:

It would be nice to be in a position to where you could have that conversation in a controlled environment versus dealing with during unfavorable circumstances, because it's hard to talk to somebody when you've got them in handcuffs. I mean, we do it all the time. I know a lot of officers and I have tried it myself over the years, but that is not a good time to do that. Because one, you do not really have that much time with them. And two, normally they are still heated over the situation. I cannot tell you how many times I've heard that "Well, I'm not mad at you, I'm mad at the situation." You know, we get that a lot, and that makes sense (PA Unidentified).

Subtheme Two: Modifying the image and perceptions of police officers

The second subtheme that followed was also the change in image and perceptions of the police officers. The participants explained how the interactions during the outreach program allowed for the civilians to see the other side, or the more open and amicable side of the police officers. Participant Three shared the common misconceptions the civilians have toward them. He highlighted how the police officers are often unappreciated and unacknowledged for their work. Therefore, the outreach program allows both parties to understand and see a better side of one another:

> We are dealing with people at their worst. Nobody ever wants... They do not want to deal with us. We are pulling them over. Well, they do not want to be pulled over. Their houses broke into. They do not want their house... We see the worst of people. You know, let us say your house is on fire, you call the fire department. That is bad, but the fire department is not taking you to jail. We are coming to take people to jail on domestics. People do not call us because they want us to come over and have dinner with them, they call us because something bad has happened. You know, and from the little thing of getting stopped because you have a taillight out, well, that can burn somebody's day
> (PA III).

Ultimately, Participant Seven also touched on the negative effects of media on the perceptions of the society on the policemen and their institution. The participant expressed how the outreach program can show a better and more positive image of the police to the community members:

I'm sorry! I'm kind of getting lost in a circle. My point was that people are not taking personal responsibility. Now, as far as our police department, we are heavily watched by the media and by groups, so our personal responsibility is held to an extremely high standard, comparatively. So, we do have to take responsibility for what we do. We are recorded in everything that we do and everything that we say. There's no getting out of what you do. You have got to be honest and you've got to be truthful, but our feet are held to the fire too, whereas the community is not. You know, we have to be responsible, the community does not. That is a huge failure, in my opinion (PA VII).

Subtheme Three: Seeing the officers as normal human beings

The third subtheme was seeing the officers as normal human beings. During a group session, Participant One narrated how he observed the change in perception of the community members toward the police officials. With the positive change, this official realized the need for both groups to cooperate and work together to fully improve the perception and trust of the civilians on the police institution:

> If you're talking about a police officer, you know, we're in uniforms. And sometimes if you get to know people, the more time you spend with them, you humanize them. You learn about them, you know. You start bridging those gaps, those culture differences, and you start seeing that, hey, you know, we're going to have our differences, but there's some things that we'll have in common with everybody.
>
> There are some things that you and I have in common, and I'll in common with him or him. We're not always going to have everything in common, but if we can bridge those gaps of the stuff, we don't have in common with the things we do have in common and understand that we're both people, and we start learning each other more. I believe that that helps build trust (PA I).

Church's Role in Helping the Outreach Program Build Trust

The second research question asked the role of the church in helping the outreach program build trust. The thematic analysis of the focus group discussions led to the generation of one major theme, four minor themes, and one subtheme. Church members indicated how the church is a strong foundation for the youth community members. The ability of the church to build and hone the youth is another factor in increasing the trust of the community members through the outreach programs. The church members believe in the effectiveness of the church and its program to mentor the youth and leading them to the right path. The police members had limited perceptions of the role of the church in helping the outreach program build trust, and thus resulted in just minor themes. Table Two contains the breakdown of the themes addressing the second research question of the study for both focus groups.

Table Two

Breakdown of the Themes Answering Research Question Two

Focus Group	Themes	Number of References
FGD One: Church Members	Building a strong foundation for the youth community members *Mentoring the youth and leading them to the right path*	5
	Creating interaction opportunities between the community members and the police department	2

	Maintaining the positive image of the police officers	4
FGD Two: Police Officers	Providing the opportunity to build relationships	3
	Building a strong foundation for the youth	4

*Note: Subtheme/s

Major Theme Three: Building a Strong Foundation for the Youth Community Members

The third major theme of the study was the role of the church in building a strong foundation for the youth. The church is believed to be a trusted source of knowledge, lessons, and values to improve the current condition and state of the youth in local communities. Participants Three, Seven, Nine, Ten, and Thirteen all shared this perception. Participant Three shared a short background on the current attitudes and behaviors of the youth today. Using Trayvon Martin's case as an example, the participant pointed at the need for the church to play a role in polishing the knowledge and attitude of the youth of today. With the improved behaviors, cases will be fewer, and negative encounters should also be eliminated over time: What I'm about to say is no way meant to minimize what happened in the Martin case. But if we are to look at the whole situation, we need to understand that Mr. Martin was a truant. He missed school a lot. He was very disrespectful to his parents, terrible student, very disrespectful not only to law enforcement but to leaders. And to be quite frank, he was almost home, and he turned around and charged back towards the person who shot him.

Now, I say all of that to say to piggyback on Number Five, I think that the role and how we can expand this is starting to plant generational seeds for those young men, young boys who are growing up in environments where there is not a solid foundational father figure. Where there is not an early opportunity to cultivate a respect for leadership and respect for women and understanding the importance of education and being a good provider, when those things are absent at home. I think that the opportunity presents itself for our outreach to start early to reach children to provide them those mentors early on that will help really bridge the gap on what they're missing so that you will have fewer instances of the Martin case or what happens at times (PA III).

Meanwhile, Participant Seven believed in the need for the institutions to reach out and help the youth with their problems and issues. Again, having Trayvon Martin as an example, the participant found the need for the church to be a trusted source of knowledge, counsel, and lessons for the youth of today through their outreach programs and activities:

When she was talking about Trayvon Martin and the things that he did, those were things I did. I was a Trayvon Martin. And I think a lot of the kids are angry, and no one is reaching the anger, because I was angry. And no one is reaching the anger. And I think you have got to talk to them, one on one, and let them know that you do care about them, and why are you angry? You are at the age where you're supposed to enjoy life. But, like me, it was me against the world, because adults didn't want to have nothing to do with me; I was too bad. And so, they did not want to help me. So... But a lot of times the anger is help me, and that is what we have to reach out to (PA VII). Participant Ten described the role of the church as the institution that "plants the seeds early." The participant shared how there is a need to build trust between the community and the church for the improvement of our youth:

And I think that was my turn, looking at—going, again, from what Number Three said—yes, we need to plant the seeds early. But then I think our role too as a congregation is to be intercessory. We start planting these seeds down here, but you got that one that Number Thirteen just spoke of. We have got to intercede somewhere in that older child's life that feels comfortable acting that way.

And I think that another role that we have is we have opened the door, we cannot unopen it. We are at a point in our society and in this trust building and community that if we don't get back to old school, and I am using this figuratively, when things happen that the kids are not having to pick their teeth up off the ground like we did, not literally... Well, literally we did. But until we get back to accountability, teaching expectation... And that's my third thing that needs to happen. You know, the second thing is we can't unopen the door. We started something here that should not be shut down.

And the third thing, if I don't lose my thought, is this trust building must grow into expectation (PA X).

Lastly, Participant Thirteen agreed with Participants Three and Ten, and discussed the need for the youth to have activities and programs on basic etiquette and expected behaviors and attitudes. Some of which are respect, accountability, and self-control:

> I'm with her, too, Number Three. Like I was telling Number Ten—we talked about it—I said, I don't, I said I'm hard on the older people, how they talk about these young kids. I'm hard on that. Because you must go back at least three generations—momma, grand momma, and great- grand momma at least that far back, to understand the origin of the problem. Because some of these kids that have the attitude that they have, and if they... We had a problem on the bus this week. And then when the police officer come to your school and you take them off that bus, then they going to pull some capital letters on the police and why he's in his face. Can you imagine what that rascal said at home to his momma or dad? And most of them mommas and then

go sit and tell the police officer, right there on the school,

crazy letters, that we can't say, in his face (PA XIII).

Only two minor themes were generated from the analysis of the

second group discussion. The police members had limited reactions

and perceptions to address the role of the church in helping the

outreach program build trust. The perceptions of providing the

opportunity to build relationships and a strong foundation for the

youth may need further research for further

validity.

Role of Police Department in Helping the Outreach Program Build Trust

The third research question was the role of the police department

in helping the outreach program build trust. The thematic analysis

of the data from the two groups led to the discovery of two major

themes, one minor theme, and three subthemes. It was then

uncovered from the discussions how the church members believe

the police department helps build trust by allowing officers to be

more visible and approachable to the community members.

Meanwhile, the police officers themselves found the need to

improve the community's perceptions of the police. This is evident, as the people are lacking appreciation for the hard work of the police. The rest of the themes are found in Table Three, addressing the third research question of the study for both the focus groups.

Table Three

Breakdown of the Themes Answering Research Question Three

Focus Group	Themes	Number of References
FGD One: Church Members	Making themselves more visible and approachable to the community members *Improving the image of the police officers* *Needing police officers of color, community members can relate to*	7
FGD Two: Police Officers	Needing to improve the community's perceptions of the police *Lacking appreciation for the hard work of the police*	4
	Creating interaction opportunities between the community members and the police department	5

Note: Subtheme/s

Major Theme Four: Making Police More Visible and Approachable to the Community Members

The fourth major theme of the study was the positive effect of making the police members more visible and approachable to the community members. More specifically, the presence of the police has improved the image of the police, while realizing the need for more police of color to enhance communication.

Participant One explained the need to know and familiarize the local community with the police officers. Additionally, being acquainted with the officers allows for a better relationship between the two groups:

> It's very essential, especially because the police officers are not coming from our community. That's why we do need to know who they are. Or, you know, I know some of them that live in my particular neighborhood are from Hendersonville, but they live in my neighborhood. I don't know them, I just see the police cars, and I see them come and go. But they don't make any attempt, like anybody else, to know the people who live around them. But that's just the society we live in; we don't really know our neighbors (PA I).

Subtheme One: Improving the image of the police officers

The first subtheme was the improvement of the police officers' overall image in the eyes of the community members. Participant Two stated how the program has made a statement and regarded the police officers as credible yet approachable. With the negative perceptions of the police officers, the church members have worked hard to work hand in hand with the officers in order to increase the community's trust:

> One of my experiences is when people feel...and it takes time to build a relationship. So, we've had some time. People don't want to bring you in if they feel like you are a threat to them or if you are going to embarrass them. So, we've demonstrated that we're nonthreatening. We can send the right people to sit on a board or to be in a community meeting that is not going to embarrass us or them but will be able to give some constructive feedback and be able to just listen and say, "Okay, now I understand what their plan is. They are having problems recruiting.

They need help finding people. Who do we know?" Then we can start helping them facilitate whatever plan they have. Or if their plan is somewhat flawed, we can say, "Hey, have you thought about this? Maybe that's not a good idea for this community." But I would think if we, if you, or someone can approach the mayor and see if there's an opportunity for us to be able to get into some of these inner circle meetings where they're talking about how they're putting together their police force and what are the needs that they have, that maybe they're having a hard time filling those positions, and then how can we help (PA II)? Participant Three added how the community leaders and institutions should work together to improve the image of the police or those in uniform. Also, it would help to be able to relate and connect with the officers:

> And while I certainly agree that diversity is reflective of our nation, we want to be able to interact with people, sometimes similar of makeup of us. But I think what's more important, in my opinion, is to improve the quality of that person (PA III).

Finally, Participant Ten explained how the church members are working together with the police officials to improve the overall image of the men in uniform. The participant even suggested some activities that could help recover the negative views of the public and gain more trust and belief about the police officers:

So, one thing that, one of the experiences here in this, both sides are, we're showing them something different than what they see every single day. Number Five brought up some things about having programs—Number Three and Five, I cannot remember—having programs that include and bring in and show them something different. Let them ride along a couple of nights a week with the police officer to see what that police officer does and encounters. Have some kind of something with the department where they go in, the kids go in for classes, and building those relationships inside the department and things, and maybe they will say, "I want to be a police officer."

I think the role of the police department is to be aware of things like we're talking about right here, and act on it. In other words, when we say okay, we don't see anybody that looks like us as a police officer. So, having that knowledge, do something that brings in folks that you wouldn't ordinarily apply for, to qualify for it, or be interested in it. You know, make it appealing, and make being a police officer appealing. Have an investment in this community (PA X).

Subtheme Two: Needing police officers of color community members can relate to:

The other subtheme that emerged was the suggestion to include police officers of color whom the community members can connect with or relate to. Participant Five believed the views of the public would improve if the police, as an institution, would be more inclusive and welcoming of people of color. The participant added that the police can gain trust if they exhibit a friendlier and accepting image:

> Okay, and I don't mean to keep laboring the point, but we were talking about trust and all that stuff. And with the inclusion from the community in leadership and police level, it's only a certain amount of trust I'm going to have for you when you keep your organization exclusive and you keep excluding me and my community. I cannot trust... Okay, I can trust as far as, hey, you're nice to me, Hey, you didn't beat me up, Hey, you didn't do this. Okay, I can trust you as far as that, but how much can I really trust

you when you won't bring me in and bring anybody from my community in, in any positions that matter or any capacities that matter? It is just, okay, hey, we can be friendly, but we are still going to keep you excluded. It's still that barrier that impedes the trust until it's more inclusive (PA V).

Meanwhile, Participant Nine agreed with Participant Five and shared his personal experience on how inclusiveness and diversity helped the locals trust those in uniform. In addition, the participant suggested the need to have more police officers of color the locals can be more comfortable to connect with:

To go along with what Number Five was saying, when I grew up there were at least two Black policemen. And every Black person in Gallatin knew those two Black policemen by name, family, and everything. You didn't go to church with them, but you still knew them. And now if I see a Black policeman, it's like, where has he been? You know, I just, occasionally, I'll see one. I don't know if they're living in Gallatin or what. But when we grew up, we had faces that we could relate to and we could walk up to and talk to, just like we would our neighbor. So, I agree with Number Five—there needs to be more policemen of color that we can relate to (PA IX).

Major Theme Five: Needing to Improve the Community's Perception of Police

The fifth major theme was the need to improve the community's perceptions of the police officers. The police members themselves shared this theme. The second group of participants reported how the police department needs to put in more effort in helping to improve the community's perception and increase the community's trust over time. One police participant admitted how they still receive negative criticism from the community. As part of the government institution, the participant believes the police and community must work together to remove the current gaps and misconceptions they may have:

> As I was saying, we're held to a higher standard and a higher accountability, which is good, because we should be. We should not be able to violate somebody's rights or do something that is against what we should do. But there

again, the community must do their part as well. We can't rely on the excuses from the sixties, seventies, or eighties of what is happening now. You know, there's got to be accountability (PA Unidentified).

Similarly, another participant added: "I'll agree with that, and say that our church's duty to step up, and maybe they need to do more, or they don't need to do more..." Finally, one participant expressed: "It's accountability. People aren't taking accountability for their own actions. They'd rather just blame it on the easiest excuse [such as] race [and] culture" (PA Unidentified).

Ecological Systems Theory's (Collaboration) Role in Helping the Outreach Program Build Trust

The fourth research question asked how the ecological systems theory (collaboration) assists in helping the outreach program build trust. Participants from both groups shared how the collaboration through the program has led to the willingness of the church and police members to collaborate and seek other ways to help one another. Both groups indicated the same major theme or the sixth and seventh major themes of the study. Table Four contains the breakdown of the results from the analysis of the data addressing the

fourth research question of the study.

Table Four

Breakdown of the Themes Answering Research Question Four

Focus Group	Themes	Number of References
FGD One: Church Members	Developing the initiative to collaborate with and help one another	3
FGD Two: Police Officers	Developing the initiative to collaborate with and help one another	4

Note: Subtheme/s

Major Theme Six: Developing the Initiative to Collaborate

with and Help One Another (Church)

The sixth major theme discussed how collaboration between the

two institutions allowed them to develop trust and work to develop

better outcomes and benefits for the local community. Participants

Two, Five, and Eleven from the church group all believed so.

Participant Two stated how the church and the police can work as

one and develop resources that can better assist the community

members, especially during the outreach program. From

transportation services to the recruitment of more members,

suggestions were formed and shared during the group: One thing I would say is we could go to the mayor and talk to the mayor about what opportunities are there for us to assist in recruitment, assist in addressing any particular issues that you may discuss with your department heads, that being the chief of police, the chief of the fire department, the other chiefs. Is there something that we can get involved with, from a citizen's base, to give input and to assist the mayor in her planning and recruitment? And as Number Five was saying, so we would know some of that inner circle information to be able to respond to it from a community base.

And maybe this is sharing our data. But you're touching fifty kids on Wednesday that live in these apartments. So, let me get you in the car, and I'm going to take you. Why don't you ride the bus with us, and you can see where we're picking them up from? So, you will see extremely specific of the sensitivity that you can have and then it becomes, "Okay, I get it" (PA II).

Meanwhile, Participant Five added that the church can also give advice and recommendations to the police department, especially when there are negative cases and backlash from the media:

One, we could be a place where we can provide them with potential employees and people in leadership positions to be on staff because we're the community. We're in the community. They can look to us, and we can refer people for them. Not only just employment, but in leadership positions, and we could serve as an advisory board or accountability board for our community.

Since we're speaking of Trayvon Martin case, when injustices do happen, we can get more of a feel, more of a way we can have some solutions. We have some advice to give to the police how to better react, how to better address these type issues, how to go about creating resolutions, and correcting and doing better in the future and preventing those type of things. And when they are in the wrong, holding them accountable (Participant Five).

Major Theme Seven: Developing the Initiative to Collaborate with and Help One Another (Police)

The final major theme was again the development of the willingness and initiative to work as one with the church members. The police members were proactive in giving suggestions to the facilitator during the FGD. One participant believed the Wednesday activity of the church could be a perfect time for the police to show their support and become available to the local community members: "No, no, you're absolutely right. The Wednesday situation, where you're bringing children into the church, are you all keeping them for two, three hours? We could actually probably ask our zone officers to stop in at that point." Correspondingly, another participant praised the effort of the church and its programs:

I say you all are doing a great job. Can you get some other people? I mean, really, seriously, you all are doing a great job. I've always enjoyed talking to you all. Everything I've asked of you all, you all have been willing to do. Like you said, when we've got a small department and we've got limited resources, you all have always been there to assist us, and I think it's worked great. I've seen the, you know, or personally reaped the benefits from it. It is about people letting us in.

Summary

The fourth chapter contained the findings from the qualitative thematic analysis of the focus group discussions with the African American church members and the Caucasian police officers. The purpose of this study was to evaluate an outreach program developed by the West Eastland Church of Christ to develop trust with the local police. The analysis led to the generation of seven major themes, all pertaining to and addressing the four research questions of the study (see Appendix D). Chapter five will expound on the findings further and discuss them in relation to the literature. Correspondingly, there commendations, implications, and conclusions are found in that chapter.

CHAPTER 5

DISCUSSION/RECOMMENDATIONS

Introduction

There is a reported increase in police injustice toward African Americans (Brunson et al., 2015). Specifically, there are increasing numbers of cases of police officers shooting unarmed African American males in the United States (Brunson et al., 2015). The church is one of the avenues to developing more trusting relationships between the police and the African American community.

The West Eastland Church of Christ outreach program in Gallatin, Tennessee, was the focus of this study. Specifically, I focused on the program's effectiveness with its goal of developing trust between church community members and the Gallatin police. With this study, I sought to discover if the program is doing what it was designed to do. What are the possibilities for the program? How can the program be improved? What are the critical factors in developing a better police-community alliance?

This outreach program evaluation helped me determine if any significant changes have taken place between the two groups. The outcomes and assessment will assist in developing short- and long-term goals for the program. The information gathered in this study will be used to enhance its strengths, correct its weaknesses, and build upon its next opportunities.

Building Trust

The first research question I addressed was how the church's outreach program has helped build trust with the police department. The first major theme I identified in the study was the church members' familiarization with the Gallatin police. In particular, participants in both focus groups expressed that a lack of familiarization might drive mistrust, while familiarization could help build trust and open communication. In fact, the majority of the church members mentioned that the outreach program allowed for establishing relationships through the familiarization of church members with the police.

The participants noted that the opportunities to communicate openly with the officers, see the officers as ordinary human beings, continue the presence and visibility of the police, and see the police officers as community models had provided the foundation for building relationships, all of which were facilitated through familiarization. Prior research confirms these results, for example:

> Not only does police force size predict lower levels of police homicide both within cities and between cities over time, suggesting that increased force size precedes increased violence as an effective form of coercive social control, but it produces substantively more interesting results when used as a dependent variable in conflict and racial threat empirical tests. (Snyder, 2013, p. 12)

My findings can best be explained by Cross's racial identity theory, which holds that the identities of people of color in the United States are predominantly shaped in five stages: pre-encounter, encounter, immersion, internationalization, and internationalization-commitment (Vandiver, Cross, Worrell, & Fhagen-Smith, 2002). It is during this final stage that people of color incorporate their identities into the broader group identity, which is predominantly African American in many communities (Vandiver et al., 2002). At the pre-encounter and encounter stages of racial identity development, the interactions between people of color and police shape how these individuals come to understand police (Vandiver et al., 2002). Specifically, according to Cross, if people of color know police officers only as coercive forces, then they will be hesitant to trust and assist police (Vandiver et al., 2002). Thus, it is at this stage that familiarization with police should begin if African American community members are to develop trust in the police and be active participants in fulfilling the public functions of police, including both the coercive and noncoercive functions (Vandiver et al., 2002).

The police recognized this need also; the officers had observed the familiarization that had taken place between the police and the church communities. The focus group discussions also highlighted participants' belief that building trust between church members and police officers required providing opportunities for the two groups to communicate and interact openly. From this perspective, communication may be the primary means of facilitating familiarization. Church members in this study indicated that the outreach program had allowed members to be much more comfortable around police officers, primarily through their increased interactions and conversations with the police. A positive consequence was understanding and viewing the police officers as rational human beings instead of people of coercion.

This finding emerged from the constant communication and interaction between the church members and officers that demonstrated that the church members' perceptions were amendable and could be transformed from skeptical to accepting, based primarily on their viewing police officers as normal humans. This finding supports an application of Cross's racial identity theory, in that it shows that African American communities can transform how they view their identities in relation to the police at the encounter stage of identity.

Another theme to emerge related to familiarization was the positive influence that the constant presence and visibility of police officers could have on members of African American communities. The establishment of both a continuous presence and visibility provided the grounds for fostering relations between the community and police officers, and presence and visibility may help establish trust. A similar theme that emerged was that the familiarization of church members with the police department provided memories for church members that served to reinforce the positive roles of police officers in the community. This may be integral to the development of Black identities in relation to the police in such communities (Cordner, 2014; Walker & Katz, 2012; Wilson, 2013). An absence of positive memories may decrease the positive long-term associations between community members and police.

I also found that the church members' images and perceptions of the police had been amendable through familiarization, positive interactions, and communication. For example, church member focus group participants explained that the interactions that occurred during the outreach program had allowed civilians at the functions to view the local police officers as more open and amicable, as demonstrating the possibility of noncoercive functions of the police in African American communities.

While Cross's theory can help explain the formation and transformation of Black racial identity in relation to police officers, the democratic theory of community policing may best explain why these positive interactions shape the image and perceptions of police officers for members of Black communities who have primarily negative memories of interactions with the police (Kappeler & Gaines, 2012).

Under the democratic theory of community policing, communities must be empowered for police functioning to be effective (Fielding, 2005). Police have a coercive role in society, but they also have a role as public servants to help build and support communities. When communities are empowered and have a voice in the functions of police in their communities, the police are going to be more focused on community building and less on coercion. By witnessing the noncoercive functions of police, African American communities can transform how they view law enforcement through both positive associations and memory formation. It is thus a combination of communication and witnessing positive, noncoercive aspects of policing that fosters these changes. Familiarization may be insufficient if interactions do not promote the image of police as performing noncoercive functions in addition to their coercive duties.

Role of the Church

The second research question I addressed was regarding the role of the West Eastland Church of Christ in helping its community-police relations outreach program build trust. The majority of the church members in that focus group felt that the church serves as a strong foundation for the youth community members, suggesting that the church and perhaps other community organizations are in the unique position to foster positive relations between Black communities and police.

The ability of the church in particular to influence the youth is another factor in increasing community trust in the police through the outreach program. In this study, the church members believed that the effectiveness of the church and its program to mentor youth were important for the church and for broader community development. In contrast, the police officers had few perceptions of the church's role in helping the outreach program build trust.

Another theme of the study involved the church's role in building a strong foundation for youth. The church members perceived the church to be a trusted source of knowledge and values to improve the current state of the youth in local communities, including involving the police in these communities. Several of the participants indicated that the church played a major role in shaping young people's knowledge and perspectives, and thus the church should play a major role in facilitating the relationships between African American communities and the police. It should be noted, however, that other community organizations may fill a similar role to that of the church in facilitating these relations. For this study I targeted the church, specifically a Church of Christ, as a vital community organ for positive change.

Role of the Police

The third research question I addressed was about the role of the police department in helping the outreach program build trust. Based on the study results, the church members shared the strong belief that the police department helps build trust through positive interactions with church members, but only by officers allowing themselves to become more visible and more approachable across the community. This requires a shift from police officers being visible in African American communities only performing coercive functions.

Moreover, police officers recognized the need to improve the community's perceptions of the police through increased approachability and more visibility in the positive, noncoercive functions they perform. Cross's racial identity theory can be applied here by recognizing that police visibility in performing noncoercive functions can provide the grounds for African American community members to recognize the positive functions of police during the pre-encounter and encounter stages of racial identity formation.

Another theme of the current study was the positive effects of increased police visibility and approachability to the church and the African American community at large. Specifically, with the present study I confirmed that the police officers' presence has improved their image in local communities. However, it was also discovered that church members would likely trust the police more if they saw greater African American representation on the police force. Thus, improving the police department's image among the church community may require ensuring that African American residents are better represented among the police force. If the Gallatin police make no other changes, greater representation of African American community residents as police officers performing noncoercive functions should increase.

Systems Theory on Collaboration

The fourth research question I addressed was how the ecological systems theory (collaboration) aided the outreach program in building trust. In the current study, participants from both the church member and police officer focus groups were willing to share information about how the collaboration through the outreach program had increased the willingness of both to collaborate and seek ways to help one another. In fact, members of both groups indicated that they recognized the need for increased collaboration for mutual benefit. In turn, however, church members want to see police officers performing more positive, primarily noncoercive functions. This would reflect the empowerment of the church under the democratic theory of community policing. Meanwhile, the police officers want to see more information sharing from the church and the African American community.

The participants in this study expected that these activities would improve the relations between the church and the police and would facilitate the development of trust between the two groups, which in turn would increase their mutual willingness to participate in such activities. For example, if the police were more active in the church programs and demonstrated noncoercive functions in the community, church members would be more willing to share information, further facilitating relationship development.

Another major theme that emerged was that the collaboration between these two institutions had revealed similarities. They both wanted to be accepted and appreciated, and both believed that the perception that the police were against the community—so-called blue versus Black—had to end. The focus group members in both groups believed that the church and law enforcement did not need to be enemies because both already faced many challenges. In fact, several participants from the church discussed how the two groups could work together to form a better community. For example, participants believed that local police could better assist the church, especially through the outreach program, in a way that would develop mutual trust. Other areas of improvement identified were more active engagement in transportation services and improved church member safety during worship and Bible classes.

Similarly, I found that the police department's willingness and initiative to work with the church was a major factor in enhancing the relationships between the police and the church community. The participants in the police focus group expressed eagerness to develop such relationships through increased involvement. Under Cross's racial identity theory, establishing such connections and relations would allow future generations of the Black community to view the police as facilitators of benefits within the community. However, this may be achievable only if the police can demonstrate to youth that they offer noncoercive functions within the community in addition to the clear coercive functions that they serve.

Limitations of the Study

The first limitation of the study relates to the characteristics of the sample. Specifically, the size of Gallatin, Tennessee, the police department, and the church were limitations: The town has a population of 30,000, the city has twenty-six police officers, and the church has 150 members, and the findings of this study might not be generalized to other populations or contexts. Although my findings are applicable within this community and may guide other communities in similar situations, more expansive and inclusive research needs to be conducted before the results are generalizable across all African American communities and police departments.

I also did not consider gender in the study. The only demographic factors I considered were race and age; both police officers and church members had to be at least eighteen. The police were all white men, and the church congregants were African American members of the predominantly Black West Eastland Church of Christ in Gallatin. Gender in the context of community police relations could add another perspective to these relationships.

Another study limitation was also that I based my evaluation only on the responses of the African American congregants and the Caucasian police officers. I had to assume that the participants were answering as honestly as possible and were not exaggerating their responses; I reminded the participants that their honest answers would be significant in understanding the experiences of both parties and evaluating the effectiveness of the outreach program. The use of focus group discussions also limited the study; this data collection strategy could not ensure whether the participants in the same group had had similar experiences. I asked follow-up questions after participants' comments and others' responses to ensure that any concerns from the other participants would be noted and brought to the attention of the group.

Recommendations

As I noted, the size of the sample in this study was a limitation; there is a need for further research from a metropolitan city with a more extensive police department and a church with more congregants. I chose my participants based on their races, but it would enhance this research to unearth how police of different races as well as genders view trust between police officers and community

members of minority groups, including how to

increase that trust.

Researchers could conduct a quantitative study to determine

whether the findings of this study could be generalized to broader

populations or a more representative sample of the populations of

police officers and African Americans or members of other minority

groups. A quantitative study could also lead to a valid instrument for

measuring the trust between police officers and African Americans.

Additionally, future researchers could include the perspectives of

church and police leaders on how the two institutions can work

together to improve mutual trust. The leaders of the church could

provide their experiences on how they guide their congregants, and

the leaders of police departments could share how they guide their

officers in treating each person with justice and fairness.

Based on the findings of the current study, interactions between

the church and police can facilitate positive relationships. The public

relations theory of policing can serve as a guide in constructing these

relationships: The thematic analysis revealed that fostering positive relations and increasing familiarization between police and the target community are major factors in building trust between these groups. According to the public relations theory of policing, improving the roles of police in communities, especially communities with low trust in the police, requires direct attempts to improve the relations between these communities and the police force (Lee & McGovern, 2013). Based on the findings of the current study, I propose the following recommendations to guide churches and police departments to enhance trust between African American communities and the police:

- Community organizations, including churches, should invite police officers to participate in community-building and relations-building events, including dinners, discussions, church services, and festivals.
- Members of the community should reach out to police officers to help solve community problems independent of criminal activity, such as community cleanup efforts and public health campaigns.

- Police departments and organizations should seek to actively participate in community events, including those hosted by predominantly African American churches and organizations.

- Police departments and organizations should establish channels of open communication that are based not on investigating crime and enforcing coercion but on fostering relationships and encouraging transparent two-way communication.

- Police officers should make efforts to familiarize themselves with leaders in African American communities, including church and community organization leaders.

- Police departments and organizations should conduct routine training exercises aimed at developing relationships within communities, enabling officers to focus more on the democratic functions of their positions rather than entirely on the coercive functions.

My above recommendations are supported by Tyler et al. (2015), who found that certain elements are needed for the police to influence positive public perceptions: public participation, neutrality, respect, and trustworthiness. Moreover, involving broad local communities in developing specific strategies for managing social order and encouraging public acceptance would lead to public buy-in (Tyler et al., 2015).

Implications

The major implication of this study was the revelation of factors that are required for the success of outreach programs aimed at bolstering relationships between the police and church community members. Such factors include establishing a visible and approachable police presence in communities, increased familiarization between community members and the police, and police demonstration of noncoercive functions in communities.

Individually, members of law enforcement and of community churches should reflect on their misconceptions about each other. The two groups need to be open-minded to be able to be sincere in their interactions during such outreach programs to pave the way for trust in their relationships; African American church congregants and police officers should collaborate with each other to improve these sometimes-volatile relationships.

The results of this study provided evidence for significant changes in the two institutions of Christian churches and law enforcement. There is initial evidence to support the effectiveness of the West Eastland Church of Christ's outreach program to develop trust between African American congregants and the police officers of Gallatin, Tennessee; I found that the two groups had positive perceptions of each other because of their interactions during outreach program activities. Members of the focus groups from both communities emphasized the need for church members and police officers to work with each other to improve the trust in their relationships. Churches and police departments could develop curricula for similar outreach programs focusing on enhanced collaboration to develop trust between police and African American communities.

Society can also benefit from the findings of this study. The initial data provided evidence of the effectiveness of the West

Eastland Church of Christ's outreach program to increase trust in the relationships between church community members and police officers in Gallatin, Tennessee. Churches and police departments can work together to better communicate and develop relationships that incorporate trust and mutual respect.

The analysis results revealed seven major themes. The first major theme of the church was the familiarization of church members with the police. The first subtheme regarding building trust between the church members and the police was the opportunity to communicate and interact openly through the outreach program. The second subtheme of the study was seeing the officers as ordinary human beings, the third was the positive influence of the constant police presence and visibility, and the last was about how the program allowed the police officers to be seen as community role models.

The second major theme was the familiarization of police with church members. The first subtheme was the police officers' opportunities to interact and communicate closely with church members, the second was the change in community members' images and perceptions of the police officers, and the third was the church community members seeing the officers as ordinary human beings. The third major theme of the study was the role of the church in building a strong foundation for the local community's youth. Two minor themes emerged under this major theme: the

first was that the police officer participants had little perspective on or knowledge regarding the church's role in helping the outreach program build trust, and the second was that more research is required on opportunities to build relationships and a strong foundation for youth.

The fourth major theme of the study was the positive effect of making the local Gallatin police more visible and approachable to the church community. The first subtheme was the church members improved overall images of the police officers, and the second was the suggestion to recruit and hire African American police officers the community members could relate to. The fifth major theme was the need to improve the community's perceptions of the police, and the sixth related to how collaboration between the two institutions allowed them to develop trust and work to create better outcomes and benefits for the local community.

The final major theme was again the police department's new willingness and initiative to work as one with the church members. The results of this study could provide positive social change given that I found that the outreach program had been effective in increasing trust in the relationships between police officers and African American community members in Gallatin, Tennessee. This increased trust could lead to a more inclusive society, which results in less discrimination against African

Americans.

Last Word

The history of policing and the African American community has had its challenges since slavery. The variables that continue to perpetuate the problems are fear, economics, and greed. I do not know which carries the strongest magnitude; however, the ongoing conflict between the blue and Black must be abridged to the point of collaboration for the community. There must be an open discussion about the role policing has played in enforcing discriminatory laws from the time of slavery until now. The community Afrocentric church must become intentional about creating outreach ministries that can include the local police community.

The concentration of this study was to evaluate a three-year-old church outreach program designed to develop trust between police and an African American church. The analysis extracted experiences that took place between the Gallatin, Tennessee, police and the West Eastland Church of Christ located in Gallatin, Tennessee. Due to the limited scope of this research, there were areas of interest that were off-limits that deserve further exploration. First, I am interested to see if there are differences in how African American police officers and female officers would respond to research questions. Second, I am curious about the role of racial identity influences answers of police and church members. Finally, I would like to see if there would be a different outcome with a metropolitan police and church.

The material will be used to build bridges between police and the African American community. They both need the other to survive. Police officers must admit that there are laws that discriminate and there are laws that they do not agree with, yet because of the oath was taken, they must enforce them. On the other hand, to envision a community without law enforcement is a total disaster. The community must show greater appreciation for the role and responsibility of the police. Police work can be a hazardous job.

Furthermore, the dream should consist of improving citizen access to police. It does not hurt for police officers to smile under their dark shades and acknowledge community individuals with a "hello." Police are to serve and protect. The service part can be enhanced by affording alternative call treatment for police dispatched to a facility. The police recognize that those members in touch through public needs are the most significant feature of community-based policing, and support training of all members of the community policing approach.

REFERENCES

The Associated Press and NORC Center for Public Affairs
Research. (2015). *Law enforcement and violence: The
divide between Black and White Americans*. Retrieved from
http://www.apnorc.org/projects/Pages/HTML%20Reports/l
aw-enforcement-and-violence-the-divide-between-
blackand-white-americans0803-9759.aspx

Bain, A., Robinson, B. K., & Conser, J. (2014). Perceptions of
policing: Improving communication in local communities.
International Journal of Police Science & Management,
16(4), 267-276. https://doi.org/10.1350/ijps.2014.16.4.345

Black, P. J., & Kari, C. J. (2010). Policing diverse communities:
Do gender and minority status make a difference? *Journal
of Ethnicity in Criminal Justice*, *8*(3), 216-229.
https://doi.org/10.1080/15377938.2010.502848

Boszormenyi-Nagy, I. (1997). Response to "Are trustworthiness
and fairness enough? Contextual family therapy and the
good family." *Journal of Marital & Family Therapy*, *23*(2),
171-173. Retrieved from
https://www.questia.com/read/1P3-11602159/response-
toare-trustworthiness-and-fairness-enough

Boyd-Franklin, N. (2013). *Black families in therapy:
Understanding the African American experience*. New
York: Guilford Publications.

Braga, A. (2003). Serious youth gun offenders and the epidemic of
youth violence in Boston. *Quantitative Criminology*,
33(19), 33-54. https://doi.org/10.1023/A:1022566628159

Bratton, W. J., & Kelling, G. L. (2015). *Why we need broken
windows policing*. Retrieved from
https://www.assumption.edu/sites/default/files/Broken%20
Windows%20Policing.pdf

Braun, V., & Clarke, V. (2014). Using thematic analysis in psychology. *Qualitative Research in Psychology, 3*(2), 77-101. doi:10.1191/1478088706qp063oa

Bronfenbrenner, U. (1977). Toward an experimental ecology of human development. *American Psychologist, 32*(7), 513531.

Bronfenbrenner, U. (1994). Ecological models of human development. In *International encyclopedia of education* (2nd ed.). Reprinted in M. Gauvin & M. Cole (Eds.), *Readings on the development of children* (2nd ed.). Oxford: Elsevier. Retrieved from http://www.psy.cmu.edu/~siegler/35bronfebrenner94.pdf

Brunson, R. K. (2007). "Police don't like black people": African American young men's accumulated police experiences*. *Criminology & Public Policy, 6*(1), 71-101. https://doi.org/10.1111/j.1745-9133.2007.00423.x

Brunson, R. K. (2015). Focused deterrence and improved police–community relations. *Criminology & Public Policy, 14*(3), 507-514. https://doi.org/10.1111/1745-9133.12141

Brunson, R. K., & Weitzer, R. (2011). Negotiating unwelcome police encounters: The intergenerational transmission of conduct norms. *Journal of Contemporary Ethnography, 40*(4), 425-456.

Brunson, R. K., Braga, A. A., Hureau, D. M., & Pegram, K. (2015). We trust you, but not that much: Examining policeblack clergy partnerships to reduce youth violence. *Justice Quarterly, 32*(6), 1006-1036. https://doi.org/10.1080/07418825.2013.868505

Cao, L., Lai, Y. L., & Zhao, R. (2012) Shades of blue: Confidence in the police in the world. *Journal of Criminal Justice, 40*, 40–49. Retrieved from https://www.researchgate.net/profile/Liqun_Cao/publicatio n/256600455_Shades_of_blue_Confidence_in_the_police_ i n_the_world/links/5a2e8894a6fdcc196d1311d7/Shades-ofblue-Confidence-in-the-police-in-the-world.pdf

Carlsen, B., & Glenton, C. (2011). What about N? A methodological study of sample-size reporting in focus group studies. *BMC Medical Research Methodology*, *11*(1), 26-35. https://doi.org/10.1186/1471-2288-11-26

Clardy, B. K. (2011). Deconstructing a theology of defiance: Black preaching and the politics of racial identity. *Journal of Church & State*, *53*(2) 203-221. Retrieved from https://www.jstor.org/stable/24708169

Combrinck-Graham, L. (2014). Being a family systems thinker: A psychiatrist's personal odyssey. *Family Process*, *53*(3), 476-488. https://doi.org/10.1111/famp.12090

Cook, R. (2013). *Sweet land of liberty: The African-American struggle for civil rights in the twentieth century*. New York: Routledge.

Cope, D. G. (2014). Methods and meanings: Credibility and trustworthiness of qualitative research. *Oncology Nursing Forum, 41*(1), 1-13. doi: 10.1188/14.ONF.89-91

Cordner, G. (2014). Community policing. In M. D. Reisig & R. J. Kane (Eds.), *The Oxford handbook of police and policing* (pp. 148-171). New York: Oxford University Press.

Crosby, B. (1986). Employee involvement: Why it fails, what it takes to succeed. *Personnel Administrator*, *31*(2), 95-107.

Cross, W. E. (1985). Black identity: Rediscovering the distinction between personal identity and reference group orientation. *Beginnings: The social and affective development of Black children*, *12*(1), 155-171. Retrieved from https://www.jstor.org/stable/41601216

Davis, I. (2012). The Black church: Not a monolith. *Diverse Issues in Higher Education, 29*(12), 19. Retrieved from https://www.questia.com/magazine/1G1-299257271/theblack-church-not-a-monolith

Desmond, M., Papachristos, A. V., & Kirk, D. S. (2016) Police violence and citizen crime reporting in the Black community. *American Sociological Review, 81*(5), 857–876. Retrieved from https://doi.org/10.1177/0003122416663494

DeYoung, C. P. (2011) The role of the Black church in the civil rights movement: Justice, peace & reconciliation - The example of Martin Luther King. *Journal of Academia.* Retrieved from https://www.academia.edu/3313352/The_Role_of_the_Black_Church_in_the_Civil_Rights_Movement?auto=download ad

Dowler, K. (2003). Media consumption and public attitudes toward crime and justice: The relationship between fear of crime, punitive attitudes, and perceived police effectiveness. *Journal of Criminal Justice and Popular Culture, 10*(2), 109-126. Retrieved from https://www.albany.edu/scj/jcjpc/vol10is2/dowler.pdf

Drake, B. (2015) *Divide between Blacks and Whites on police runs deep.* Washington, DC: Pew Research Center. Retrieved from http://www.pewresearch.org/facttank/2015/04/28/blacks-whites-police/

Fielding, N. G. (2005). Concepts and theory in community policing. *The Howard Journal of Criminal Justice, 44*(5), 460-472. https://doi.org/10.1111/j.1468-2311.2005.00391.x

Fraser, M. W., Richman, J. M., & Galinsky, M. J. (2009). *Intervention research: Developing social programs.* New York: Oxford University Press.

Fusch, P. I., & Ness, L. R. (2015). Are we there yet? Data saturation in qualitative research. *The Qualitative Report, 20*(9), 1408.

Govier, T. (1997). *Social trust and human communities*. Montreal, Canada: McGill-Queen's University Press.

Govier, T. (1998). *Dilemmas of trust*. Montreal, Canada: McGillQueen's University Press.

Hardin, R. (2002). *Trust and trustworthiness*. New York: Russell Sage Foundation.

Hartwig, M. C. (2000). Programming: Nuts and bolts. *New Directions for Student Services, 90*, 45.

Holton, R. (1994). Deciding to trust, coming to believe. *Australasian Journal of Philosophy, 72*(1), 63–76. https://doi.org/10.1080/00048409412345881

Houghton, C., Casey, D., Shaw, D., & Murphy, K. (2013). Rigour in qualitative case-study research. *Nurse Researcher, 20*(4), 12-17. doi:10.7748/nr2013.03.20.4.12. e326

Johnson, K. E. (2004). Police-Black community relations in postwar Philadelphia: Race and criminalization in urban social spaces, 1945-1960. *Journal of African American History, 89*(2), 118-134. doi:10.2307/4134096

Jones, K. (1996). Trust as an affective attitude. *Ethics, 107*, 4–25. Retrieved from http://www.cridaq.uqam.ca/IMG/pdf/Jones_K._1996._Trust_as_an_Affective_Attitude_Daniel_Weinstock.pdf

Kappeler, V. E., & Gaines, L. K. (2012). *Community policing: A contemporary perspective*. New York and Oxford: Routledge.

Karakurt, G., & Silver, K. E. (2014). Therapy for childhood sexual abuse survivors using attachment and family systems theory orientations. *The American Journal of Family Therapy, 42*(1), 79-91. https://doi.org/10.1080/01926187.2013.772872

Kitzinger J. (1994). The methodology of focus groups: The importance of interaction between research participants. *Sociology of Health & Illness, 16*(1):103–121. https://doi.org/10.1111/1467-9566.ep11347023

Kuhn, K. (2000). Problems and benefits of requirements gathering with focus groups: A case study. *International Journal of Human-Computer Interaction, 12*(3/4), 309-325. https://doi.org/10.1080/10447318.2000.9669061

La Vigne, N., Fontaine, J., & Dwivedi, A. (2017). How do people in high-crime, low-income communities view the police? Washington, DC: Urban Institute. https://www.urban.org/sites/default/files/publication/88476/ how_do_people_in_high-crime_view_the_police.pdf

Lee, M., & McGovern, A. (2013). *Policing and media: Public relations, simulations and communications*. Oxon, UK: Routledge.

Leedy, P. D., & Ormrod, J. E. (2016). *Practical research: Planning and design*. Boston: Pearson.

Lincoln, C. E., & Mamiya, L. H. (1990). *The black church in the African American experience*. Durham, NC: Duke University Press.

Lincoln, Y. S., & Guba, E. G. (1985). *Naturalistic inquiry*. Thousand Oaks, CA: SAGE Publications.

Lowe, J. S., & Shipp, S. C. (2014). Black church and Black college community development corporations: Enhancing the public sector discourse. *Western Journal of Black Studies, 38*(4), 244-259. Retrieved from

https://web.a.ebscohost.com/abstract?direct=true&profile=
e
host&scope=site&authtype=crawler&jrnl=01974327&AN
=
100700658&h=OPpnlm%2fmV8BmaFhBOKi0pfgJ2GRPo
RPwHnk3wPapnNYk5HePQblEyoNdJzzt1cMJ1PMrXMX
GrDulQM1E0iS6hA%3d%3d&crl=c&resultNs=AdminWe
bAuth&resultLocal=ErrCrlNotAuth&crlhashurl=login.aspx
%3fdirect%3dtrue%26profile%3dehost%26scope%3dsite%
26authtype%3dcrawler%26jrnl%3d01974327%26AN%3d
1 00700658

Lurigio, A. J., Greenleaf, R. G., & Flexon, J. L. (2009). Effects of race on relationships with the police: A survey of African American and Latino youths in Chicago. *Western Criminology Review*, *10*(1), 29–41. Retrieved from http://www.westerncriminology.org/documents/WCR/v10n 1/Lurigio.pdf

MacDonald, J., & Stokes, R. J. (2006). Race, social capital, and trust in the police. *Urban Affairs Review*, *41*(3), 358-375. https://doi.org/10.1177/1078087405281707

Major, C., & Savin-Baden, M. (2010). Exploring the relevance of qualitative research synthesis to higher education research and practice. *London Review of Education*, *8*(2), 127–140. Retrieved from http://www.ingentaconnect.com/content/ioep/clre/2010/000 00008/00000002/art00004?crawler=true

Mertens, D. M. (2014). *Research and evaluation in education and psychology: Integrating diversity with quantitative, qualitative, and mixed methods.* Thousand Oaks, CA: SAGE.

Miles, M. B., Huberman, A. M., & Saldana, J. (2014). *Qualitative data analysis: A methods sourcebook* (3rd ed). Thousand Oaks, CA: SAGE.

Minuchin, S. (1974). Families and family therapy. Cambridge, MA: Harvard University Press.

Moore, G. A., & Neiderhiser, J. M. (2014). Behavioral genetic approaches and family theory. *Journal of Family Theory & Review, 6*(1), 18-30. https://doi.org/10.1111/jftr.12028

Muijs, D. D. (2004). *Doing quantitative research in education with SPSS*. London: SAGE Publications.

National Institute of Justice. (2016). *Race, trust and police legitimacy*. Washington, DC: National Institute of Justice. Retrieved from: https://www.nij.gov/topics/lawenforcement/legitimacy/Pages/welcome.aspx

Nelsen, H. M., & Nelsen, A. K. (1975). *Black church in the sixties*. Lexington, KY: University of Kentucky Press.

Office of Community Oriented Policing Services (COPS). (2009). *Building trust between the police and the citizens they serve*. Washington, DC: U.S. Department of Justice. Retrieved   from: https://www.justice.gov/crs/file/836486/download

COPS. (2015). *The President's Task Force on 21st Century Policing implementation guide: Moving from recommendations to action*. Washington, DC: U.S. Department of Justice. Retrieved from http://noblenational.org/wpcontent/uploads/2017/02/President-Barack-Obama-Task-Force-on-21st-Century-Policing-Implementation-Guide.pdf

Pickett, X. (2007). Policing Black communities. *Public Justice, 30*(1), 1-4. Retrieved from https://www.cpjustice.org/uploads/Policing_Black_Communities.pdf

Pringle, J., Drummond, J., McLafferty, E., & Hendry, C. (2011). Interpretative phenomenological analysis: A discussion and critique. *Nurse Researcher, 18(3), 20-24.* doi:10.7748/nr2011.04.18.3.20.c8459

Rosa, E. M., & Tudge, J. (2013). Urie Bronfenbrenner's theory of human development: Its evolution from ecology to bioecology. *Journal of Family Theory & Review*, 5(4), 243-258. https://doi.org/10.1111/jftr.12022

Rubenstein, E. S. (2017). *The color of crime.* Oakton, VA: New Century Foundation. Retrieved from https://2kpcwh2r7phz1nq4jj237m22-wpengine.netdnassl.com/wp-content/uploads/2016/03/Color-Of-Crime2016.pdf

Savin-Baden, M., & Major, C. (2013) *Qualitative research: The essential guide to theory and practice.* London: Routledge.

Scriven, M. (1996). Types of evaluation and types of evaluator. *Evaluation Practice, 17*(2), 151-61. https://doi.org/10.1177/109821409601700207

Sharp, E. B., & Johnson, P. E. (2009). Accounting for variation in distrust of local police. *Justice Quarterly, 26*(1), 157-182.

Silverman, D. (Ed.). (2016). *Qualitative research.* Thousand Oaks, CA: SAGE.

Simpson, T. W. (2012). What is trust? *Pacific Philosophical Quarterly, 93*(4), 550-569. https://doi.org/10.1111/j.1468-0114.2012.01438.x

Skocpol, T. (2013). *Diminished democracy: From membership to management in American civic life* (Vol. 8). Norman, OK: University of Oklahoma Press.

Snyder, B. (2013). *Policing the police: Conflict theory and police violence in a racialized society* (Doctoral dissertation). University of Washington. Retrieved from https://digital.lib.washington.edu/researchworks/bitstream/handle/1773/22805/Snyder_washington_0250O_11356.pdf?sequence=1

Sorsa, M. A., Kiikkala, I., & Åstedt-Kurki, P. (2015). Bracketing as a skill in conducting unstructured qualitative interviews. *Nurse Researcher, 22*(4), 8-12. doi:10.7748/nr.22.4.8.e1317

Stoutland, S. E. (2001). The multiple dimensions of trust in resident/police relations in Boston. *Journal of Research in Crime and Delinquency, 38*(3), 226-256. https://doi.org/10.1177/0022427801038003002

Trader-Leigh, K (2008) *Understanding the role of African American churches and clergy in community crisis response.* Washington, DC: Health Policy Institute. Retrieved from http://jointcenter.org/sites/default/files/UnderstandingRoleofChurches.pdf

Tyler, T. R. (2005). Policing in black and white: Ethnic group differences in trust and confidence in the police. *Police Quarterly, 8*(3), 322-342. https://doi.org/10.1177/1098611104271105

Tyler, T. R., Goff, P.A., & MacCoun, R. J. (2015) The impact of psychological science on policing in the United States: Procedural justice, legitimacy, and effective law enforcement. *Psychological Science in the Public Interest, 16*(3). 75-109. Retrieved from http://www.psychologicalscience.org/publications/policing.html

Van Craen, M., & Skogan, W. G. (2014). Differences and similarities in the explanation of ethnic minority groups' trust in the police. *European Journal of Criminology, 8*, 267–285. https://doi.org/10.1177/1477370814535375

Vandiver, B. J., Cross, W. E., Worrell, F. C., & Fhagen-Smith, P. E. (2002). Validating the Cross Racial Identity Scale. *Journal of Counseling Psychology, 49*(1), 71-84. doi:10.1037//0022-0167.49.1.71

Walker, S., & Katz, C. M. (2012). *The police in America: An introduction.* New York: McGraw-Hill.

Weitzer, R., & Tuch, S. A. (2008) Police-community relations in a majority-Black city. *Journal of Research in Crime and Delinquency, 45*(4). 398-428. Retrieved from http://www.skogan.org/files/Police_Community_Relations _in_a_Majority_Black_City.pdf

Williams, D. N. (2012). What I learned about Churches of Christ and Christian Churches/Churches of Christ. *StoneCampbell Journal, 15*(2), 165-176.

Wilson, J. M. (2013). *Community Policing in America.* New York: Routledge.

Yancy, G., & Jones, J. (Eds.). (2013). Introduction. *Pursuing Trayvon Martin: Historical contexts and contemporary manifestations of racial dynamics* (pp. 1-24). Lanham, MD: Lexington Books.

Yin, R. (2014). *Case study research: Design and methods* (5th ed.). Thousand Oaks, CA: SAGE.

Young, J. L., Griffith, E. E., & Williams, D. R. (2014). The integral role of pastoral counseling by African American clergy in community mental health. *Psychiatric Services, 54*(5), 688–692. https://doi.org/10.1176/appi.ps.54.5.688

Appendix A Interview Questions

- What does trust mean to you?
- How has this outreach program-built trust?
- What are the strengths of this program?
- How can the strengths be built upon?
- What are the weaknesses of this program?
- What are the reasons for the weaknesses of the program?
- What are the possibilities for this program?
- What are other collaborative activities the two groups can do to build trust?
- How would you say the police/church feel about the outreach program?
- What experiences do you share that are similar to the police/similar to the church members?
- What are your final thoughts as we conclude the group?

To inquire about bulk purchases
or speaking engagements,

Please contact:
Benjamin Roberts III
BRJ Publishers/Purposed Life
broberts@apurposedlife.com
(615) 241-9020

www.ingramcontent.com/pod-product-compliance
Lightning Source LLC
Chambersburg PA
CBHW070916270326
41927CB00011B/2588